HOW TO MOVE TO LIE(
A COMPREHENSIVE GUIDE
BY
WILLIAM JONES
2024

How to Move to Liechtenstein: A Comprehensive Guide by William Jones
This book edition was created and published by Mamba Press
©MambaPress 2024. All Rights Reserved.

Contents

Preface
  Introduction
  Chapter 1: Getting to Know Liechtenstein: An Overview
  Chapter 2: Planning Your Move: Where to Start
  Chapter 3: Understanding Residency Requirements
  Chapter 4: Finding Accommodation: From Apartments to Chalets
  Chapter 5: Navigating Healthcare: Your Guide to the Healthcare System
  Chapter 6: Education and Schools: Options for Families
  Chapter 7: Employment and Business Opportunities
  Chapter 8: Learning the Language: German in Liechtenstein
  Chapter 9: Cultural Etiquette and Social Customs
  Chapter 10: Banking and Financial Matters
  Chapter 11: Transportation: Getting Around Liechtenstein
  Chapter 12: Exploring Liechtenstein's Natural Beauty
  Chapter 13: Outdoor Activities: Hiking, Skiing, and More
  Chapter 14: Festivals and Celebrations: Embracing Local Traditions
  Chapter 15: Dining and Cuisine: A Taste of Liechtenstein
  Chapter 16: Shopping and Markets: Where to Shop
  Chapter 17: Entertainment and Nightlife
  Chapter 18: Sports and Recreation: Staying Active in Liechtenstein
  Chapter 19: Volunteering and Community Engagement
  Chapter 20: Socializing and Making Friends
  Chapter 21: Religious Practices and Places of Worship
  Chapter 22: Legal Matters: Understanding the Law
  Chapter 23: Taxes and Financial Planning
  Chapter 24: Climate and Weather: What to Expect
  Chapter 25: Safety and Emergency Services
  Chapter 26: Pet Ownership: Guidelines and Regulations
  Chapter 27: Day Trips and Excursions: Exploring the Region
  Chapter 28: Sustainable Living: Environmental Initiatives
  Chapter 29: Maintaining a Work-Life Balance
  Chapter 30: Dealing with Homesickness and Culture Shock
  Chapter 31: Respecting Wildlife and Nature Conservation
  Chapter 32: Celebrating Diversity: Expat Communities in Liechtenstein
  Conclusion
  Appendix

Preface

Welcome to the land of castles, mountains, and a charming blend of tradition and modernity—Liechtenstein. Whether you're dreaming of an Alpine adventure or contemplating a fresh start in a new country, this guide is your ticket to navigating the ins and outs of moving to Liechtenstein.

I'm William Jones, your travel companion on this journey. As a seasoned traveler and expat, I understand the excitement and challenges that come with relocating to a new place. My goal is to arm you with all the information you need to make your move to Liechtenstein as smooth and rewarding as possible.

Why Liechtenstein, you may ask? Well, for starters, this tiny principality packs a punch when it comes to natural beauty. Picture-perfect villages, rolling hills, and majestic peaks—Liechtenstein is a postcard come to life. But it's not just the scenery that's captivating; Liechtenstein's rich history, vibrant culture, and strong economy make it an attractive destination for those seeking a high quality of life.

But before you pack your bags and head for the hills, there are a few things you need to know. From navigating residency permits to finding a place to call home and immersing yourself in the local culture, moving to Liechtenstein requires careful planning and preparation. That's where this guide comes in.

Over the next few pages, we'll delve into everything you need to know about making the move to Liechtenstein. We'll cover the practicalities of finding a place to live, getting to grips with the healthcare system, and understanding the local customs and etiquette. But we'll also explore the fun stuff—like where to go hiking, the best spots for après-ski, and how to make friends with the locals.

Moving to a new country can be a daunting prospect, but it's also an incredible opportunity for personal growth and adventure. So, whether you're moving for work, study, or just a change of scenery, I hope this guide will help you make the most of your time in Liechtenstein.

So, grab your passport, pack your sense of adventure, and let's dive into the enchanting world of Liechtenstein. Your new life awaits!

Introduction

Welcome to the breathtaking principality of Liechtenstein, a hidden gem nestled in the heart of Europe. If you've ever dreamed of living in a fairytale setting surrounded by snow-capped mountains, lush green valleys, and quaint villages straight out of a storybook, then Liechtenstein is the place for you.

But Liechtenstein is more than just a pretty postcard. Despite its small size—it's one of the smallest countries in the world—this tiny principality punches well above its weight in terms of culture, history, and economic stability. From its medieval castles perched atop rocky crags to its thriving business sector and world-class ski resorts, Liechtenstein offers a little something for everyone.

So, why choose Liechtenstein as your new home? Well, for starters, there's the stunning natural scenery. Whether you're an avid hiker, a skiing enthusiast, or simply someone who enjoys a leisurely stroll in the great outdoors, Liechtenstein's landscape has something to offer. Picture yourself traversing winding mountain trails, breathing in the crisp Alpine air, and marveling at panoramic views that stretch as far as the eye can see.

But Liechtenstein isn't just for nature lovers. History buffs will delight in exploring the country's rich heritage, from its medieval castles and ancient ruins to its charming museums and art galleries. And if you're a foodie, you're in for a treat—Liechtenstein may be small, but it boasts a surprisingly diverse culinary scene, with everything from hearty Alpine fare to gourmet delicacies.

Of course, no discussion of Liechtenstein would be complete without mentioning its thriving economy. Despite its landlocked location and lack of natural resources, Liechtenstein has managed to carve out a niche for itself as a global financial hub. With low taxes, a business-friendly environment, and a highly skilled workforce, it's no wonder that companies from around the world are flocking to set up shop here.

But perhaps the most compelling reason to move to Liechtenstein is the quality of life it offers. With its low crime rate, excellent healthcare system, and strong sense of community, Liechtenstein is a place where you can truly put down roots and build a fulfilling life for yourself and your family.

Of course, moving to a new country is never easy. There are visas to apply for, language barriers to overcome, and cultural differences to navigate. But fear not—this guide is here to help. Over the following pages, we'll walk you through everything you need to know about making the move to Liechtenstein, from obtaining residency permits to finding accommodation, getting to grips with the local healthcare system, and integrating into the community.

So, whether you're a seasoned expat or embarking on your first international adventure, I invite you to join me on a journey of discovery as we explore the enchanting world of Liechtenstein. Your new life awaits!

Chapter 1

Getting to Know Liechtenstein: An Overview

Welcome to Liechtenstein, the charming principality nestled in the heart of Europe. Despite being one of the smallest countries in the world, Liechtenstein boasts a rich tapestry of history, culture, and natural beauty that will capture your heart from the moment you arrive.

Situated between Switzerland and Austria, Liechtenstein is often overlooked by travelers in favor of its larger neighbors. But those who take the time to explore this tiny gem will be rewarded with breathtaking Alpine vistas, quaint villages straight out of a storybook, and a warm welcome from the friendly locals.

One of the first things you'll notice about Liechtenstein is its size. Covering just 160 square kilometers, this tiny principality is roughly the same size as Washington, D.C. Despite its small stature, however, Liechtenstein is home to around 39,000 people, making it one of the most densely populated countries in the world.

Liechtenstein is also one of the last remaining remnants of the Holy Roman Empire, with a history that dates back over a thousand years. The principality was established in 1719 by the merger of two smaller territories, and it has been ruled by the same family—the Princely House of Liechtenstein—ever since.

Today, Liechtenstein is a constitutional monarchy with a parliamentary democracy, meaning that while the royal family still holds symbolic power, the day-to-day running of the country is handled by elected officials. The current ruler, Prince Hans-Adam II, is one of the wealthiest monarchs in the world, thanks in large part to the family's extensive art collection and investments in banking and industry.

Despite its small size, Liechtenstein boasts a thriving economy, with a strong emphasis on finance, manufacturing, and tourism. The country is known for its favorable tax laws and business-friendly environment, which have attracted companies from around the world to set up shop here. In fact, Liechtenstein has one of the highest GDP per capita rates in the world, making it one of the wealthiest countries in terms of income per person.

But Liechtenstein isn't just about business and finance. The principality is also home to a rich cultural heritage that reflects its position at the crossroads of Europe. From its medieval castles and Baroque churches to its charming villages and vibrant arts scene, Liechtenstein offers a wealth of cultural experiences for visitors to enjoy.

One of the best ways to experience Liechtenstein's rich cultural heritage is by exploring its many museums and galleries. The principality is home to a surprising number of cultural institutions, including the Liechtenstein National Museum, which offers a fascinating glimpse into the country's history and heritage, and the Kunstmuseum Liechtenstein, which showcases contemporary art from around the world.

Of course, no visit to Liechtenstein would be complete without exploring its stunning natural beauty. The principality is blessed with some of the most spectacular scenery in Europe, from soaring mountain peaks to lush green valleys and crystal-clear lakes. Whether you're an avid hiker, a skiing enthusiast, or simply someone who enjoys a leisurely stroll in the great outdoors, Liechtenstein has something to offer.

But perhaps the most enchanting thing about Liechtenstein is its people. Warm, welcoming, and proud of their heritage, the locals are always eager to share their love for their country with visitors. Whether you're chatting with a shopkeeper in Vaduz or enjoying a meal at a local restaurant, you'll find that the people of Liechtenstein are always happy to make you feel at home.

So, whether you're planning a weekend getaway or considering a more permanent move, I invite you to explore all that Liechtenstein has to offer. From its stunning natural beauty to its rich cultural heritage and thriving economy, this tiny principality is truly a hidden gem waiting to be discovered. Welcome to Liechtenstein—your adventure starts here!

Chapter 2
Planning Your Move: Where to Start

Congratulations on making the decision to move to Liechtenstein! Whether you're drawn to the country's stunning natural beauty, thriving economy, or rich cultural heritage, one thing's for sure—you're in for an adventure. But before you can start exploring your new home, there's a lot of planning and preparation to do. From obtaining the necessary visas to finding a place to live and everything in between, moving to Liechtenstein requires careful consideration and attention to detail. But fear not—this chapter is here to help you get started on the right foot.

The first step in planning your move to Liechtenstein is determining your eligibility to live and work in the country. As a non-EU citizen, you'll need to obtain a residence permit before you can take up residence in Liechtenstein. The specific requirements for obtaining a residence permit vary depending on your nationality, the purpose of your stay, and other factors. Generally speaking, however, you'll need to have a valid reason for moving to Liechtenstein, such as employment, study, or family reunification, and you'll need to provide proof of sufficient financial means to support yourself during your stay.

Once you've determined your eligibility for a residence permit, the next step is to familiarize yourself with the various types of permits available and the application process. Liechtenstein offers several different types of residence permits, including permits for employees, students, self-employed individuals, and retirees, each with its own set of requirements and procedures. Depending on your circumstances, you may need to submit additional documentation, such as a job offer letter, proof of enrollment in a recognized educational institution, or evidence of sufficient funds to support yourself without needing to work.

In addition to obtaining a residence permit, you'll also need to consider other practicalities such as finding a place to live, arranging healthcare coverage, and opening a bank account. Finding accommodation in Liechtenstein can be challenging, particularly in popular areas such as Vaduz and Schaan, so it's a good idea to start your search as early as possible. Whether you're looking for a cozy apartment in the city center or a spacious chalet in the mountains, there are plenty of options available to suit every taste and budget. Be sure to consider factors such as location, amenities, and proximity to public transportation when choosing your new home.

Healthcare coverage is another important consideration when planning your move to Liechtenstein. While Liechtenstein has a high-quality healthcare system, it's essential to ensure that you have adequate coverage to protect yourself in case of illness or injury. If you're coming from a country with a reciprocal healthcare agreement with Liechtenstein, you may be eligible for coverage under the country's national health insurance scheme. Otherwise, you'll need to arrange private health insurance coverage before you arrive.

Opening a bank account in Liechtenstein is relatively straightforward, but it's important to choose the right bank and account type to suit your needs. Liechtenstein is known for its strong banking sector, with a wide range of financial institutions offering a variety of services tailored to expatriates and international clients. Whether you're looking for a basic checking account for day-to-day transactions or a comprehensive wealth management package, there's sure to be a banking solution that meets your needs.

In addition to these practical considerations, it's also important to take the time to research and familiarize yourself with the local customs, culture, and language before you arrive. While English is widely spoken in Liechtenstein, particularly in business and tourist areas, knowing some basic German phrases can go a long way in helping you to integrate into the local community and make new friends. Similarly, understanding the local customs and etiquette will help you to navigate social situations with confidence and respect.

Moving to a new country is never easy, but with careful planning and preparation, your move to Liechtenstein can be a smooth and rewarding experience. By taking the time to familiarize yourself with the requirements and procedures for obtaining a residence permit, finding accommodation, arranging healthcare coverage, and opening a bank account, you'll be well on your way to making Liechtenstein your new home. So, roll up your sleeves, get organized, and start planning your move today—your adventure awaits!

Chapter 3
Understanding Residency Requirements

So, you've decided to make the move to Liechtenstein—congratulations! Now it's time to tackle one of the most important aspects of your relocation: understanding the residency requirements. As a non-EU citizen, obtaining a residence permit is essential for living and working in Liechtenstein legally. In this chapter, we'll delve into the various types of residence permits available, the eligibility criteria, and the application process, so you can navigate the residency requirements with confidence.

First and foremost, it's crucial to determine your eligibility for a residence permit in Liechtenstein. The specific requirements vary depending on your nationality, the purpose of your stay, and other factors. Generally speaking, however, you'll need to have a valid reason for moving to Liechtenstein, such as employment, study, family reunification, or investment, and you'll need to meet certain financial criteria to support yourself during your stay.

One of the most common types of residence permits in Liechtenstein is the residence permit for employees. If you've secured a job offer from a Liechtenstein-based employer, you may be eligible for this type of permit. To qualify, you'll typically need to demonstrate that you have a valid employment contract, sufficient qualifications and experience for the position, and proof of adequate financial means to support yourself and any dependents during your stay.

Another popular option is the residence permit for students. If you've been accepted into a recognized educational institution in Liechtenstein, you may be eligible for this type of permit. To qualify, you'll need to provide proof of enrollment in a full-time course of study, evidence of sufficient funds to cover your living expenses, and proof of adequate health insurance coverage.

Family reunification is another common basis for obtaining a residence permit in Liechtenstein. If you have a spouse, registered partner, or close family member who is a Liechtenstein citizen or holds a valid residence permit, you may be eligible to join them in Liechtenstein. To qualify, you'll typically need to provide proof of your relationship, evidence of adequate housing, and proof of sufficient financial means to support yourself and any dependents during your stay.

In addition to these types of residence permits, Liechtenstein also offers permits for self-employed individuals, retirees, and investors, each with its own set of requirements and procedures. Whether you're planning to start your own business, retire in the Alpine paradise of Liechtenstein, or invest in the country's thriving economy, there's sure to be a residence permit that meets your needs.

Once you've determined your eligibility for a residence permit, the next step is to familiarize yourself with the application process. The specific requirements and procedures vary depending on the type of permit you're applying for, but generally speaking, you'll need to submit an application form along with supporting documentation such as your passport, proof of accommodation, proof of financial means, and any other documents required by the authorities.

It's important to note that the processing time for residence permit applications can vary depending on the volume of applications and the complexity of your case. In some cases, it may take several weeks or even months to receive a decision on your application, so it's important to plan ahead and submit your application well in advance of your planned move date.

Once you've been granted a residence permit, you'll need to fulfill certain obligations to maintain your legal status in Liechtenstein. This may include registering your address with the local authorities, renewing your permit before it expires, and complying with any conditions or restrictions attached to your permit, such as restrictions on employment or residency.

In summary, understanding the residency requirements is a crucial step in planning your move to Liechtenstein. By familiarizing yourself with the various types of residence permits available, the eligibility criteria, and the application process, you can navigate the residency requirements with confidence and ensure a smooth transition to your new life in Liechtenstein. So, roll up your sleeves, gather your documents, and start the application process today—your adventure awaits!

Chapter 4

Finding Accommodation: From Apartments to Chalets

Finding the perfect place to call home is one of the most exciting—and sometimes daunting—parts of moving to a new country. Fortunately, Liechtenstein offers a wide range of accommodation options to suit every taste and budget, from cozy city apartments to spacious mountain chalets. In this chapter, we'll explore the ins and outs of finding accommodation in Liechtenstein, so you can settle into your new home with ease.

One of the first decisions you'll need to make when searching for accommodation in Liechtenstein is whether you want to live in a city or a rural area. The capital city of Vaduz is a popular choice for many expatriates, thanks to its central location, excellent amenities, and vibrant cultural scene. Here, you'll find a variety of accommodation options ranging from modern apartments in the city center to historic townhouses nestled along cobblestone streets.

If you prefer a quieter, more laid-back lifestyle, you may opt to live in one of Liechtenstein's charming villages or rural communities. Places like Schaan, Triesenberg, and Balzers offer a peaceful retreat from the hustle and bustle of city life, with stunning mountain views and easy access to outdoor recreational activities.

Once you've decided on the location, it's time to start your search for accommodation. Fortunately, there are plenty of resources available to help you find your dream home in Liechtenstein. Online real estate websites like ImmobilienScout24, ImmoScout, and Homegate allow you to search for properties by location, size, and price range, making it easy to find options that meet your criteria.

In addition to online resources, it's also worth reaching out to local real estate agents and property management companies for assistance with your search. These professionals have intimate knowledge of the local housing market and can help you find properties that may not be listed online. They can also provide valuable advice and guidance throughout the rental process, from negotiating terms and conditions to handling paperwork and contracts.

When it comes to choosing the type of accommodation that's right for you, it's important to consider factors such as size, amenities, and budget. Apartments are a popular choice for many expatriates, offering convenience, affordability, and a wide range of amenities such as onsite parking, laundry facilities, and fitness centers. Whether you're looking for a cozy studio apartment or a spacious penthouse suite, you're sure to find options that suit your needs in Liechtenstein.

If you prefer a bit more space and privacy, you may opt to rent a house or villa instead. These standalone properties offer more room to spread out and often come with additional amenities such as gardens, patios, and private parking. Houses and villas are particularly popular in rural areas, where you'll find plenty of options nestled among the rolling hills and picturesque landscapes of Liechtenstein.

For those seeking the ultimate Alpine retreat, renting a chalet or mountain cabin may be the perfect option. These rustic yet charming properties offer unparalleled views of the surrounding mountains and valleys, as well as easy access to hiking, skiing, and other outdoor activities. Whether you're looking for a cozy cabin for a romantic getaway or a spacious chalet for a family vacation, you'll find plenty of options to choose from in Liechtenstein.

Of course, finding the perfect accommodation is just the first step in settling into your new home in Liechtenstein. Once you've found a property that meets your needs, you'll need to negotiate terms and conditions with the landlord, sign a rental agreement, and arrange for utilities and other services to be connected. It's also a good idea to familiarize yourself with the local rental laws and regulations to ensure that you understand your rights and responsibilities as a tenant.

In summary, finding accommodation in Liechtenstein is a rewarding experience that offers a wide range of options to suit every lifestyle and budget. Whether you prefer the convenience of city living, the tranquility of rural life, or the charm of a mountain chalet, you're sure to find the perfect place to call home in this beautiful Alpine principality. So, start your search today and get ready to embark on the next chapter of your adventure in Liechtenstein!

Chapter 5
Navigating Healthcare: Your Guide to the Healthcare System

Taking care of your health is a top priority, especially when moving to a new country. Fortunately, Liechtenstein boasts a high-quality healthcare system that provides comprehensive care to residents and visitors alike. In this chapter, we'll explore everything you need to know about navigating the healthcare system in Liechtenstein, from accessing medical services to understanding insurance coverage and staying healthy while living in the principality.

One of the first things you'll need to familiarize yourself with when navigating the healthcare system in Liechtenstein is the concept of compulsory health insurance. Like many other countries in Europe, Liechtenstein has a mandatory health insurance system that ensures all residents have access to essential medical care. Whether you're a citizen, a permanent resident, or a temporary visitor, you'll need to have health insurance coverage to access healthcare services in Liechtenstein.

There are two main types of health insurance in Liechtenstein: basic health insurance (Grundversicherung) and supplementary health insurance (Zusatzversicherung). Basic health insurance covers essential medical services such as doctor visits, hospital stays, and prescription medications, while supplementary health insurance provides additional coverage for services not covered by the basic insurance plan, such as dental care, alternative medicine, and private hospital rooms.

If you're employed in Liechtenstein, you'll typically be enrolled in the country's mandatory health insurance scheme through your employer. Contributions to the health insurance scheme are deducted directly from your salary, with both you and your employer sharing the cost of premiums. If you're self-employed or not employed in Liechtenstein, you'll need to arrange health insurance coverage through a private insurance provider.

In addition to compulsory health insurance, Liechtenstein also offers a range of private healthcare services for those seeking more personalized care or additional treatment options. Private healthcare providers in Liechtenstein offer a wide range of services, including specialist consultations, diagnostic tests, elective surgeries, and wellness treatments. While private healthcare services can be more expensive than those covered by basic health insurance, they often provide faster access to care and more personalized attention.

When it comes to accessing healthcare services in Liechtenstein, you'll find a range of options available to suit your needs. The country boasts a network of public and private hospitals, clinics, and medical practices, as well as pharmacies, rehabilitation centers, and specialist treatment facilities. Whether you need a routine check-up, emergency care, or specialized treatment, you'll find a wealth of healthcare providers ready to assist you in Liechtenstein.

In the event of a medical emergency, you can dial 144 to reach the emergency services in Liechtenstein. The emergency services are staffed by highly trained medical professionals who can provide immediate assistance and arrange for transportation to the nearest hospital if necessary. It's important to note that emergency medical treatment in Liechtenstein is covered by the compulsory health insurance scheme, so you won't need to worry about upfront costs in the event of an emergency.

In addition to emergency care, Liechtenstein also offers a range of preventive healthcare services to help you stay healthy and well. From routine screenings and vaccinations to health education and lifestyle counseling, there are plenty of resources available to support your health and wellbeing in Liechtenstein. Whether you're looking to quit smoking, manage a chronic condition, or simply adopt a healthier lifestyle, you'll find plenty of support and guidance from healthcare professionals in Liechtenstein.

In summary, navigating the healthcare system in Liechtenstein is a straightforward and streamlined process that ensures all residents have access to high-quality medical care. Whether you're covered by the mandatory health insurance scheme or have opted for private insurance, you'll find a wealth of healthcare providers and services available to meet your needs. So, take care of your health, stay informed about your insurance coverage, and don't hesitate to seek medical assistance if you need it—your health is your most valuable asset, and Liechtenstein is committed to helping you protect it.

Chapter 6
Education and Schools: Options for Families

Moving to a new country with children in tow can be an exciting yet daunting prospect. Fortunately, Liechtenstein offers a range of educational options to suit every family's needs, from public schools to private international schools and everything in between. In this chapter, we'll explore the education system in Liechtenstein and the various schooling options available to families, so you can make informed decisions about your children's education and ensure a smooth transition to life in the principality.

One of the first things you'll need to consider when it comes to education in Liechtenstein is the country's compulsory schooling requirement. In Liechtenstein, children are required to attend school from the age of six until they reach the age of 15 or complete their primary education, whichever comes first. This means that if you're moving to Liechtenstein with school-age children, you'll need to enroll them in a local school unless you plan to homeschool them.

Liechtenstein's education system is divided into several stages, including primary education (Grundstufe), secondary education (Sekundarstufe I and Sekundarstufe II), and tertiary education (Hochschule). Primary education typically lasts for six years and is followed by three years of lower secondary education and three years of upper secondary education. After completing secondary education, students have the option to pursue further education at a vocational school, university, or other tertiary institution.

For families looking to enroll their children in the local school system, Liechtenstein offers a network of public schools that provide free education to all residents. These schools follow the Liechtenstein curriculum and are overseen by the Ministry of Education, Culture, and

Sport. Public schools in Liechtenstein are known for their high academic standards, small class sizes, and emphasis on individualized learning, making them a popular choice for many families.

In addition to public schools, Liechtenstein also boasts a number of private schools that offer alternative educational approaches and cater to a diverse range of learning styles and preferences. Private schools in Liechtenstein may follow international curricula such as the International Baccalaureate (IB) or offer specialized programs in areas such as music, art, or sports. While private schools typically charge tuition fees, they often provide smaller class sizes, enhanced resources, and a more personalized approach to education.

One of the most popular options for expatriate families in Liechtenstein is the International School Rheintal (ISR), located in nearby Buchs, Switzerland. The ISR offers a bilingual education in English and German, with a strong emphasis on academic excellence, global citizenship, and personal development. The school follows the IB curriculum and provides a supportive and multicultural learning environment for students from diverse backgrounds.

Another option for international families is the Liechtensteinisches Gymnasium, a secondary school located in Vaduz that offers a bilingual education in German and English. The Gymnasium provides a rigorous academic program that prepares students for university and beyond, with a focus on critical thinking, creativity, and cultural awareness. The school also offers a range of extracurricular activities, including sports, arts, and community service projects.

For families with younger children, Liechtenstein also offers a number of childcare and preschool options to help prepare children for formal schooling. These include daycare centers, nursery schools, and kindergarten programs that provide a safe and nurturing environment for children to learn, play, and socialize with their peers. Many of these programs follow the Montessori or Waldorf educational philosophies, which emphasize hands-on learning, creativity, and individualized instruction.

In summary, Liechtenstein offers a range of educational options to suit every family's needs, from public schools to private international schools and everything in between. Whether you choose to enroll your children in the local school system, opt for a private school, or explore alternative educational approaches, you can rest assured that your children will receive a high-quality education that prepares them for success in the globalized world. So, take the time to research your options, visit schools, and consider your children's individual needs and preferences—your children's education is one of the most important investments you'll ever make, and Liechtenstein is committed to helping you make it a success.

Chapter 7
Employment and Business Opportunities

As you settle into life in Liechtenstein, you may find yourself exploring the employment and business opportunities available in this dynamic principality. Despite its small size, Liechtenstein boasts a thriving economy with a diverse range of industries and sectors, making it an attractive destination for job seekers, entrepreneurs, and investors alike. In this chapter, we'll delve into the employment landscape in Liechtenstein, from job opportunities and work culture to starting a business and thriving in the local economy.

One of the first things you'll notice about Liechtenstein is its strong economy, which is driven by a combination of manufacturing, finance, and tourism. Despite its landlocked location and lack of natural resources, Liechtenstein has managed to carve out a niche for itself as a global leader in industries such as precision engineering, electronics, and financial services. The country's strategic location at the heart of Europe, coupled with its business-friendly environment and skilled workforce, has attracted companies from around the world to set up operations here.

For job seekers, Liechtenstein offers a range of employment opportunities across a variety of industries and sectors. Whether you're an engineer, a banker, a software developer, or a marketing professional, you'll find plenty of job openings to suit your skills and experience in Liechtenstein. Popular job sectors in Liechtenstein include finance and banking, manufacturing, technology, healthcare, and tourism, with opportunities available at all levels, from entry-level positions to senior management roles.

One of the key advantages of working in Liechtenstein is the country's strong economy and low unemployment rate, which means there are plenty of opportunities for career advancement and professional development. In addition to competitive salaries and benefits, many employers in Liechtenstein offer perks such as flexible working hours, training and development programs, and opportunities for international travel and collaboration.

In addition to traditional employment opportunities, Liechtenstein also offers a range of options for entrepreneurs and small business owners looking to start or expand their ventures. The principality boasts a favorable business climate, with low taxes, minimal bureaucracy, and a supportive regulatory environment that makes it easy to set up and operate a business here. Whether you're launching a tech startup, opening a boutique hotel, or starting a family-run restaurant, Liechtenstein offers plenty of resources and support to help you succeed.

One of the key advantages of starting a business in Liechtenstein is the country's well-developed infrastructure and access to international markets. Liechtenstein is strategically located in the heart of Europe, with excellent transportation links and proximity to major business hubs such as Zurich, Munich, and Milan. This makes it easy to connect with customers, suppliers, and partners across Europe and beyond, helping your business to reach new heights of success.

In addition to its strong economy and favorable business climate, Liechtenstein also offers a range of incentives and support programs to help entrepreneurs and small business owners thrive. These include grants and subsidies for innovation and research, access to financing and venture capital, and support services such as mentoring, networking, and business incubation. Whether you're a seasoned entrepreneur or a first-time business owner, you'll find plenty of resources and support to help you grow your venture in Liechtenstein.

Of course, thriving in the local economy in Liechtenstein requires more than just a strong business plan and a competitive product or service. It also requires a deep understanding of the local culture, customs, and business practices. Networking and relationship-building are key to success in Liechtenstein, so take the time to get to know your colleagues, partners, and customers, and invest in building strong, long-lasting connections that will help your business succeed in the long term.

In summary, Liechtenstein offers a wealth of employment and business opportunities for job seekers, entrepreneurs, and investors alike. Whether you're looking for a rewarding career in finance, manufacturing, or technology, or dreaming of starting your own business and being your own boss, Liechtenstein has something to offer. With its strong economy, favorable business climate, and supportive ecosystem for entrepreneurship, Liechtenstein is the perfect place to launch your next career or business venture. So, roll up your sleeves, seize the opportunity, and get ready to make your mark in Liechtenstein's vibrant economy.

Chapter 8

Learning the Language: German in Liechtenstein

As you embark on your journey to Liechtenstein, you'll quickly discover that German is the primary language spoken in this picturesque principality. While many residents also speak English, particularly in urban areas and tourist destinations, having a basic understanding of German can greatly enhance your experience and help you to connect with the local culture and community. In this chapter, we'll explore the importance of learning German in Liechtenstein, as well as some tips and resources to help you master the language.

German is the official language of Liechtenstein, and it's spoken by the majority of the population in both formal and informal settings. While there are several dialects of German spoken in Liechtenstein, including Alemannic and Walser, Standard German is the language of education, government, and business, making it essential for anyone living or working in the principality to have a basic understanding of the language.

Learning German in Liechtenstein is not only practical—it's also a great way to immerse yourself in the local culture and connect with the people around you. Whether you're ordering food at a local restaurant, asking for directions on the street, or striking up a conversation with a neighbor, knowing some basic German phrases can help you to navigate everyday situations with ease and confidence.

Fortunately, there are plenty of resources available to help you learn German in Liechtenstein, regardless of your current level of proficiency. Language schools and private tutors offer a range of courses and programs tailored to learners of all ages and abilities, from absolute beginners to advanced speakers. Whether you prefer group classes, one-on-one instruction, or online learning, you'll find plenty of options to suit your needs and preferences.

In addition to formal language instruction, there are also plenty of opportunities to practice your German skills outside of the classroom. Joining local clubs and community groups, attending cultural events and festivals, and participating in language exchange programs are all great ways to immerse yourself in the language and culture of Liechtenstein while making new friends and connections along the way.

One of the best ways to learn German in Liechtenstein is to practice speaking and listening to the language in everyday situations. Take every opportunity to engage with native speakers, whether it's chatting with your neighbors, ordering groceries at the market, or attending a local language meetup. Don't be afraid to make mistakes—learning a new language is all about trial and error, and the more you practice, the more confident and proficient you'll become.

In addition to speaking and listening, it's also important to practice reading and writing in German to build your vocabulary and grammar skills. Reading newspapers, books, and websites in German, writing emails and messages in the language, and using language learning apps and websites are all effective ways to improve your reading and writing skills and reinforce what you've learned in your language classes.

If you're struggling to find the motivation to learn German, remember that mastering a new language opens up a world of opportunities, both personally and professionally. Not only will it enhance your travel experiences and allow you to connect with people from different cultures, but it can also improve your cognitive function, boost your career prospects, and enrich your overall quality of life.

In summary, learning German in Liechtenstein is not only practical—it's also a rewarding and enriching experience that will enhance your life in countless ways. Whether you're living and working in Liechtenstein or simply visiting as a tourist, having a basic understanding of German will help you to navigate everyday situations with ease, connect with the local culture and community, and make the most of your time in this beautiful Alpine principality. So, don't be afraid to dive in, make mistakes, and embrace the journey of learning a new language—you'll be glad you did!

Chapter 9
Cultural Etiquette and Social Customs

As you immerse yourself in the vibrant culture of Liechtenstein, it's important to familiarize yourself with the local customs and social etiquette to ensure a smooth and respectful interaction with the people around you. While Liechtenstein shares many cultural similarities with its neighboring countries, it also has its own unique traditions and customs that reflect its rich history and Alpine heritage. In this chapter, we'll explore some key aspects of cultural etiquette and social customs in Liechtenstein, helping you to navigate social situations with confidence and respect.

Greetings and Politeness: In Liechtenstein, greetings are an important part of social interaction, and it's customary to greet people with a handshake and a friendly "Guten Tag" (Good day) or "Grüezi" (Hello) when you meet them for the first time. When addressing someone, it's polite to use their title and last name until you're invited to use their first name. Additionally, it's considered respectful to use formal titles such as "Herr" (Mr.) or "Frau" (Mrs.) when addressing someone you don't know well, especially in professional or formal settings.

Punctuality: Punctuality is highly valued in Liechtenstein, and it's important to arrive on time for social engagements, business meetings, and appointments. Being late without a valid reason is considered rude and disrespectful, so make sure to plan your schedule accordingly and allow extra time for unexpected delays.

Dining Etiquette: Dining plays a central role in Liechtenstein's social culture, and it's common for people to gather for meals with family and friends. When dining out or attending a social event, it's customary to wait for the host or the most senior person to begin eating before you start. It's also polite to keep your hands visible on the table and to say "Guten Appetit" (Enjoy your meal) before you start eating.

When toasting, make sure to make eye contact with the other person and clink glasses gently, avoiding crossing arms with others.

Gift Giving: Giving gifts is a common practice in Liechtenstein, particularly during holidays, birthdays, and other special occasions. When giving a gift, it's thoughtful to choose something of high quality and to present it with sincerity and humility. If you're invited to someone's home for a meal or a social gathering, bringing a small gift such as flowers, wine, or chocolates is a nice gesture of appreciation for the hospitality.

Respect for Nature: Liechtenstein is known for its stunning natural landscapes, and the people of Liechtenstein have a deep respect for the environment. When exploring the outdoors, it's important to follow Leave No Trace principles and to respect wildlife, plants, and natural habitats. Additionally, it's customary to greet fellow hikers and outdoor enthusiasts with a friendly nod or "Grüezi" as you pass them on the trails.

Socializing: Liechtensteiners are known for their warm and welcoming hospitality, and socializing plays a central role in the country's culture. Whether you're attending a local festival, a community event, or a casual get-together with friends, it's important to be open, friendly, and respectful in your interactions with others. Taking the time to engage in conversation, listen actively, and show genuine interest in others will help you to build meaningful connections and foster positive relationships within the community.

Religion and Tradition: Religion holds a significant place in Liechtenstein's culture, with the majority of the population identifying as Roman Catholic. While religion plays a central role in many aspects of life in Liechtenstein, including holidays, festivals, and social customs, the country is also known for its religious tolerance and respect for diversity. Whether you're participating in a religious ceremony or attending a cultural event, it's important to be respectful of the beliefs and traditions of others, even if they differ from your own.

Language and Communication: While many residents of Liechtenstein speak English fluently, particularly in urban areas and tourist destinations, knowing some basic German phrases can greatly enhance your ability to communicate and connect with the local community. Taking the time to learn a few key phrases, such as greetings, thank yous, and simple questions, shows respect for the local language and culture and can help you to navigate everyday situations with ease.

In summary, navigating cultural etiquette and social customs in Liechtenstein is all about showing respect, humility, and appreciation for the traditions and values of the local community. By familiarizing yourself with the customs outlined in this chapter and approaching social interactions with an open mind and a willingness to learn, you'll be well-equipped to engage with the people of Liechtenstein in a respectful and meaningful way. So, embrace the opportunity to immerse yourself in the rich cultural tapestry of Liechtenstein, and enjoy the warm hospitality and genuine camaraderie of its people.

Chapter 10
Banking and Financial Matters

As you settle into life in Liechtenstein, you'll find that the principality is not only known for its stunning landscapes and rich cultural heritage but also for its thriving banking and financial sector. With its stable economy, favorable tax policies, and strict privacy laws, Liechtenstein has long been a popular destination for international investors, businesses, and individuals seeking to manage their wealth and assets. In this chapter, we'll explore the ins and outs of banking and financial matters in Liechtenstein, helping you to navigate the world of finance with confidence and ease.

Banking System: Liechtenstein is home to a robust and sophisticated banking system that offers a wide range of services to clients from around the world. The country's banks are known for their stability, reliability, and discretion, making them a popular choice for high-net-worth individuals, corporations, and trusts seeking to safeguard their assets and investments.

Private Banking: Liechtenstein is renowned for its private banking services, which cater to the needs of wealthy individuals and families looking for personalized financial solutions and wealth management advice. Private banks in Liechtenstein offer a range of services, including investment management, estate planning, tax optimization, and asset protection, tailored to the unique needs and objectives of each client.

Offshore Banking: Liechtenstein is also a leading offshore banking jurisdiction, offering a range of offshore banking services to clients seeking to diversify their assets and minimize their tax liabilities. Offshore banks in Liechtenstein provide a high level of privacy and confidentiality, making them an attractive option for individuals and businesses looking to protect their wealth and assets from prying eyes.

Fintech Innovation: In recent years, Liechtenstein has emerged as a hub for fintech innovation, with a growing number of startups and companies leveraging technology to disrupt the traditional banking and financial services sector. From blockchain and cryptocurrency to digital banking and payment solutions, Liechtenstein is at the forefront of fintech innovation, offering opportunities for investors and entrepreneurs to participate in this rapidly evolving industry.

Regulatory Environment: Liechtenstein has a well-regulated financial sector overseen by the Financial Market Authority (FMA), which is responsible for supervising and regulating banks, insurance companies, asset managers, and other financial institutions operating in the principality. The FMA ensures that banks and financial institutions adhere to strict compliance standards and anti-money laundering regulations, providing clients with confidence and peace of mind.

Taxation: Liechtenstein is known for its favorable tax policies, including low corporate and personal income tax rates, making it an attractive destination for individuals and businesses looking to minimize their tax burden. The principality also offers a range of tax incentives and exemptions for foreign investors and entrepreneurs, further enhancing its appeal as a financial hub.

Currency: The official currency of Liechtenstein is the Swiss Franc (CHF), which is used for all financial transactions and business dealings in the principality. The Swiss Franc is known for its stability and strength, making it a reliable currency for residents and visitors alike.

Opening a Bank Account: Opening a bank account in Liechtenstein is a relatively straightforward process, with many banks offering online account opening services for international clients. To open a bank account, you'll typically need to provide identification documents, proof of address, and information about the source of funds. Some banks may also require a minimum deposit or a reference from a trusted source.

International Banking Services: In addition to traditional banking services, many banks in Liechtenstein also offer a range of international banking services, including multi-currency accounts, offshore investment funds, and cross-border payment solutions. These services are designed to meet the needs of clients with international interests and facilitate seamless global transactions.

In summary, banking and financial matters in Liechtenstein are characterized by stability, discretion, and innovation, making the principality an attractive destination for investors, businesses, and individuals seeking to manage their wealth and assets. Whether you're looking for personalized wealth management services, offshore banking solutions, or access to fintech innovation, Liechtenstein offers a wealth of opportunities to meet your financial needs and objectives. So, embrace the opportunity to explore the world of banking and finance in Liechtenstein, and take advantage of the principality's unique offerings to secure your financial future with confidence and peace of mind.

Chapter 11
Transportation: Getting Around Liechtenstein

Nestled in the heart of Europe, Liechtenstein may be small in size, but it's big on charm and accessibility. As you explore this enchanting principality, you'll find that getting around is a breeze, thanks to its well-developed transportation network and compact size. In this chapter, we'll delve into the various transportation options available in Liechtenstein, helping you to navigate the principality with ease and convenience.

1. **Public Transportation**: Liechtenstein boasts a reliable and efficient public transportation system that makes it easy to travel within the principality and to neighboring countries. Buses are the primary mode of public transport in Liechtenstein, with a network of routes connecting major towns and villages throughout the country. The bus system is operated by LIEmobil, and tickets can be purchased from the driver or at ticket machines located at bus stops.
2. **Biking and Walking**: With its compact size and scenic landscapes, Liechtenstein is a paradise for cyclists and walkers. The principality offers a network of well-maintained cycling and hiking trails that wind through picturesque villages, lush forests, and rolling hills. Whether you're exploring the Rhine Valley, traversing the Alpine foothills, or meandering through the charming streets of Vaduz, biking and walking are enjoyable and eco-friendly ways to get around Liechtenstein.
3. **Car Rental**: Renting a car is another convenient option for getting around Liechtenstein, particularly if you're looking to explore the countryside or visit remote areas not accessible by

public transportation. Several car rental companies operate in Liechtenstein, offering a range of vehicles to suit your needs and preferences. With its well-maintained roads and scenic drives, Liechtenstein is a joy to explore by car, allowing you to discover hidden gems and off-the-beaten-path destinations at your own pace.

4. **Taxis**: Taxis are readily available in Liechtenstein, providing convenient door-to-door transportation for travelers and residents alike. Taxi stands can be found in major towns and tourist areas, or you can simply flag down a taxi on the street. Taxis in Liechtenstein are metered, and fares are regulated by the government, ensuring transparency and fairness for passengers. Whether you need a ride to the airport, a lift to your hotel, or a designated driver for a night out, taxis offer a convenient and reliable transportation option in Liechtenstein.

5. **Ridesharing**: While ridesharing services such as Uber are not widely available in Liechtenstein, there are alternative ridesharing platforms and apps that operate in the principality, providing travelers with additional options for getting around. These ridesharing services connect passengers with local drivers who are willing to provide rides for a fee, offering a flexible and convenient transportation solution for those looking to explore Liechtenstein without the hassle of driving or navigating public transportation.

6. **Trains**: Although Liechtenstein itself does not have its own railway system, the principality is well-connected to neighboring Switzerland and Austria by train. The Swiss Federal Railways (SBB) and Austrian Federal Railways (ÖBB) operate regular train services to and from Liechtenstein, with stops at nearby stations such as Buchs in Switzerland and Feldkirch in Austria. From these stations,

travelers can easily transfer to buses or taxis to reach their final destination in Liechtenstein.

7. **Boating**: While Liechtenstein is landlocked and does not have direct access to the sea, it is bordered by the majestic Rhine River, offering opportunities for boating and water-based activities. Several companies in neighboring Switzerland and Austria offer boat tours and cruises along the Rhine, allowing travelers to experience the beauty of the river and its surrounding landscapes from a unique perspective.

In summary, getting around Liechtenstein is a breeze, thanks to its efficient public transportation system, well-maintained roads, and compact size. Whether you prefer to explore by bus, bike, car, or foot, you'll find plenty of options to suit your needs and preferences in this charming Alpine principality. So, pack your bags, hit the road, and get ready to discover the beauty and charm of Liechtenstein—from its quaint villages and rolling hills to its majestic mountains and crystal-clear rivers, there's something for everyone to enjoy in this hidden gem of Europe.

Chapter 12
Exploring Liechtenstein's Natural Beauty

Liechtenstein may be one of the smallest countries in the world, but don't let its size fool you—this tiny principality is home to some of the most breathtaking natural landscapes in Europe. From towering mountains and lush forests to picturesque valleys and crystal-clear rivers, Liechtenstein's natural beauty is sure to captivate and inspire travelers of all ages. In this chapter, we'll embark on a journey to explore the diverse and pristine wilderness of Liechtenstein, uncovering hidden gems and must-see attractions along the way.

The Rhine River: One of Liechtenstein's most iconic natural landmarks is the majestic Rhine River, which forms the country's western border with Switzerland. The Rhine River is not only a source of scenic beauty but also a hub of outdoor recreational activities, including boating, fishing, and swimming. Visitors can take leisurely boat tours along the river, marveling at the stunning scenery and panoramic views of the surrounding mountains and valleys.

The Alps: Liechtenstein is nestled in the heart of the Alps, offering unparalleled opportunities for hiking, mountaineering, and alpine adventures. The principality is surrounded by towering peaks and rugged mountain ranges, including the picturesque Rätikon, Silvretta, and Alvier groups. Whether you're a seasoned mountaineer or a casual hiker, there are trails and routes to suit every skill level and interest, leading you through alpine meadows, past pristine lakes, and to breathtaking viewpoints overlooking the valley below.

Vaduz: The Capital City: While Liechtenstein is renowned for its natural beauty, its capital city, Vaduz, also boasts its fair share of scenic spots and green spaces. Visitors can explore the tranquil Stadtpark, a picturesque park located in the heart of Vaduz, where they can stroll along winding pathways, admire colorful flowerbeds, and enjoy panoramic views of the surrounding mountains. The park is also home to several sculptures and art installations, adding to its charm and allure.

The Three Sisters: For those seeking a more adventurous outdoor experience, the Three Sisters are a must-visit destination in Liechtenstein. Located in the southern part of the country near the town of Triesen, the Three Sisters are a trio of distinctive rock formations that rise dramatically from the valley floor, offering stunning views and photo opportunities. Hiking trails lead visitors to the base of the rock formations, where they can marvel at their sheer size and geological beauty up close.

Gaflei: The Gateway to the Alps: Situated high above the village of Triesenberg, the picturesque hamlet of Gaflei is known as the "Gateway to the Alps" and offers breathtaking views of the surrounding mountains and valleys. Visitors can hike or drive to Gaflei, where they'll find a cozy mountain hut serving traditional Alpine cuisine and refreshments. From Gaflei, adventurous hikers can continue on to explore the nearby peaks and trails, immersing themselves in the pristine wilderness of the Alps.

The Prince's Way: For a truly immersive outdoor experience, consider hiking the Prince's Way, a scenic trail that winds its way through the length of Liechtenstein, from north to south. The Prince's Way offers hikers the opportunity to explore the diverse landscapes and natural beauty of the principality, passing through picturesque villages, verdant meadows, and rugged mountain terrain along the way. Whether you tackle the entire trail or just a section of it, the Prince's Way promises unforgettable views and memorable experiences at every turn.

In summary, Liechtenstein's natural beauty is a treasure trove waiting to be discovered, with pristine wilderness, scenic landscapes, and outdoor adventures awaiting travelers at every turn. Whether you're exploring the tranquil banks of the Rhine River, scaling the towering peaks of the Alps, or hiking the length of the Prince's Way, you'll find endless opportunities to connect with nature and experience the beauty and wonder of Liechtenstein's great outdoors. So, lace up your hiking boots, pack your camera, and get ready to embark on an unforgettable journey through the natural splendor of Liechtenstein.

Chapter 13
Festivals and Celebrations: Embracing Local Traditions

One of the best ways to immerse yourself in the vibrant culture and rich heritage of Liechtenstein is by experiencing its festivals and celebrations. Throughout the year, the principality comes alive with a colorful array of events, ranging from traditional folk festivals and music concerts to cultural exhibitions and culinary extravaganzas. In this chapter, we'll explore some of the most popular festivals and celebrations in Liechtenstein, giving you a glimpse into the country's lively and diverse cultural scene.

National Day: One of the most important and widely celebrated holidays in Liechtenstein is National Day, which takes place on August 15th each year. National Day commemorates the birthday of Prince Franz Joseph II, who ruled the principality from 1938 to 1989, and is marked by a series of festive events and activities. The day typically begins with a ceremonial mass at Vaduz Cathedral, followed by a parade through the streets of Vaduz, live music performances, traditional dances, and fireworks displays. National Day is a time for Liechtensteiners to come together to celebrate their national identity and cultural heritage with pride and joy.

Liechtenstein Carnival: The Liechtenstein Carnival, or Fasnacht, is a lively and colorful celebration that takes place in the weeks leading up to Lent. During Carnival season, towns and villages across the principality come alive with music, dancing, and elaborate parades featuring elaborate costumes, colorful floats, and masked revelers. The highlight of the Carnival festivities is the traditional "Gumpiger Donnerstag" (Fat Thursday) parade, where locals don elaborate costumes and masks to chase away the spirits of winter and usher in the arrival of spring with merriment and laughter.

Vaduz Summer Nights: Throughout the summer months, Vaduz comes alive with the sounds of music and the aroma of delicious food during the Vaduz Summer Nights festival. This annual event features a series of open-air concerts, street performances, and culinary delights, showcasing the best of local and international talent. Visitors can enjoy live music ranging from jazz and blues to rock and classical, sample gourmet cuisine from food stalls and vendors, and soak up the festive atmosphere under the stars.

Liechtenstein Music Festival: Music lovers won't want to miss the Liechtenstein Music Festival, a world-class event that brings together renowned musicians and performers from around the globe. Held annually in various venues across the principality, the Liechtenstein Music Festival features a diverse lineup of concerts, recitals, and masterclasses, covering a wide range of musical genres and styles. Whether you're a classical music aficionado, a jazz enthusiast, or a fan of contemporary sounds, you'll find something to delight and inspire you at the Liechtenstein Music Festival.

Alpabfahrt: One of the most picturesque and unique traditions in Liechtenstein is the Alpabfahrt, or cattle drive, which takes place in the late summer or early autumn. During the Alpabfahrt, farmers in the mountainous regions of Liechtenstein bring their cattle down from the alpine pastures to the valley floor after spending the summer grazing in the high meadows. The cattle are adorned with colorful floral wreaths and bells, and the procession is accompanied by music, dancing, and festivities as locals and visitors alike celebrate the end of the grazing season and the safe return of the animals to the village.

Christmas Markets: The holiday season in Liechtenstein is a magical time of year, with festive Christmas markets popping up in towns and villages across the principality. These charming markets feature twinkling lights, fragrant evergreen wreaths, and stalls selling handmade gifts, ornaments, and seasonal treats. Visitors can sip mulled wine, sample traditional holiday delicacies, and browse for unique souvenirs while soaking up the festive atmosphere and enjoying live music and entertainment.

In summary, festivals and celebrations are an integral part of life in Liechtenstein, offering travelers a unique opportunity to experience the country's rich cultural heritage and vibrant community spirit. Whether you're dancing in the streets during Carnival, enjoying a summer concert under the stars, or marveling at the spectacle of the Alpabfahrt, you'll find plenty of reasons to celebrate and embrace local traditions in this charming Alpine principality. So, mark your calendar, join the festivities, and create unforgettable memories as you immerse yourself in the colorful tapestry of Liechtenstein's cultural scene.

Chapter 14
Dining and Cuisine: A Taste of Liechtenstein

Embarking on a culinary journey through Liechtenstein is like uncovering a hidden treasure trove of flavors, where traditional Alpine cuisine meets modern gastronomy in a delightful fusion of taste and tradition. From hearty mountain specialties to elegant fine dining experiences, Liechtenstein offers a diverse and vibrant culinary scene that is sure to tantalize the taste buds of even the most discerning travelers. In this chapter, we'll explore the rich culinary heritage of Liechtenstein and introduce you to some of the must-try dishes and dining experiences that await you in this charming Alpine principality.

Alpine Specialties: Liechtenstein's cuisine is deeply rooted in its Alpine heritage, with hearty mountain specialties taking center stage on menus across the principality. One of the most beloved dishes in Liechtenstein is käsknöpfle, a hearty pasta dish made with small dumplings, melted cheese, and caramelized onions. Another popular Alpine dish is rösti, crispy shredded potatoes served with a variety of toppings such as cheese, bacon, or fried eggs. These comforting and satisfying dishes are perfect for fueling up after a day of outdoor adventure in the mountains.

Local Ingredients: Liechtenstein's cuisine is characterized by its use of fresh, locally sourced ingredients, with an emphasis on quality and seasonality. The principality boasts fertile valleys, lush meadows, and crystal-clear rivers, providing an abundance of fresh produce, dairy products, and meats for local chefs and home cooks alike. Look for dishes featuring ingredients such as alpine cheeses, wild mushrooms, venison, and freshwater fish, all of which showcase the natural bounty of Liechtenstein's landscapes.

Fine Dining: For those seeking a more refined dining experience, Liechtenstein offers a number of upscale restaurants and gourmet eateries where you can indulge in haute cuisine prepared with skill and creativity. From innovative tasting menus to elegant à la carte offerings, these establishments showcase the best of local and international culinary trends, often with a modern twist. Whether you're celebrating a special occasion or simply looking to treat yourself to an unforgettable meal, you'll find plenty of options to satisfy your palate and elevate your dining experience in Liechtenstein.

Farmers' Markets: One of the best ways to experience the flavors of Liechtenstein is by visiting a local farmers' market, where you can sample and purchase fresh produce, artisanal cheeses, homemade breads, and other delicious treats straight from the source. Farmers' markets are held regularly in towns and villages throughout the principality, offering visitors the opportunity to connect with local producers, learn about traditional farming methods, and discover the true essence of Liechtenstein's culinary heritage.

Wine and Spirits: While Liechtenstein may be small in size, it boasts a burgeoning wine industry that produces high-quality wines from vineyards nestled in the Rhine Valley. Visitors can sample a variety of locally produced wines, including crisp whites, fruity rosés, and robust reds, at vineyards and wineries across the principality. In addition to wine, Liechtenstein is also known for its traditional fruit brandies, known as obstler, made from locally grown fruits such as apples, pears, and plums. These artisanal spirits are the perfect way to cap off a delicious meal or toast to a memorable evening in Liechtenstein.

Cafés and Bakeries: No culinary journey through Liechtenstein would be complete without a visit to one of its charming cafés or bakeries, where you can indulge in freshly brewed coffee, decadent pastries, and mouthwatering desserts. Whether you're craving a flaky croissant, a creamy slice of cake, or a warm apple strudel, you'll find plenty of tempting treats to satisfy your sweet tooth in Liechtenstein's cozy cafés and bakeries. Sit back, relax, and savor the moment as you enjoy a taste of Liechtenstein's rich culinary heritage in a warm and welcoming atmosphere.

In summary, dining in Liechtenstein is a feast for the senses, where traditional Alpine flavors, fresh local ingredients, and modern culinary techniques come together to create a culinary experience that is as diverse as it is delicious. Whether you're savoring hearty mountain specialties, indulging in fine dining fare, or sampling local wines and spirits, you'll find plenty of opportunities to delight your palate and nourish your soul in this charming Alpine principality. So, come hungry, explore with an open mind, and prepare to embark on a culinary adventure that will leave you craving more of Liechtenstein's mouthwatering delights.

Chapter 15
Dining and Cuisine: A Taste of Liechtenstein

In the heart of Europe, where the majestic Alps meet the serene Rhine Valley, Liechtenstein offers a culinary journey unlike any other. Despite its small size, this Alpine principality boasts a rich and diverse culinary scene that reflects its cultural heritage and natural bounty. From hearty mountain fare to elegant fine dining, Liechtenstein's cuisine is a delightful fusion of tradition, innovation, and local flavors. Join us as we embark on a gastronomic adventure through Liechtenstein, sampling its most iconic dishes and exploring the unique dining experiences that await travelers in this charming Alpine destination.

Alpine Comfort Food: Liechtenstein's cuisine is deeply rooted in its Alpine heritage, with hearty and comforting dishes that are perfect for warming up on a chilly mountain evening. One of the most beloved dishes in Liechtenstein is käsknöpfle, a savory pasta dish made with small dumplings, melted cheese, and caramelized onions. This satisfying comfort food is often served with a side of crispy bacon or a fresh green salad, making it a favorite among locals and visitors alike.

Rösti: Another Alpine favorite is rösti, a crispy and delicious potato dish that is popular throughout Switzerland and Liechtenstein. Made from grated potatoes that are fried until golden brown and crispy, rösti is often served as a side dish or as the star of the meal, topped with melted cheese, a fried egg, or a dollop of sour cream. Simple yet satisfying, rösti is the perfect accompaniment to any meal and a must-try for anyone visiting Liechtenstein.

Fresh and Local: Liechtenstein's cuisine places a strong emphasis on fresh, locally sourced ingredients, with an abundance of produce, dairy products, and meats available from the principality's fertile valleys and alpine meadows. Look for dishes featuring alpine cheeses, wild mushrooms, venison, and freshwater fish, all of which showcase the natural bounty of Liechtenstein's landscapes and reflect the seasonal rhythms of the region.

Fine Dining: For those seeking a more refined dining experience, Liechtenstein offers a number of upscale restaurants and gourmet eateries that combine traditional Alpine flavors with modern culinary techniques. From innovative tasting menus to elegant à la carte offerings, these establishments showcase the best of local and international cuisine, often with a focus on seasonal and locally sourced ingredients. Whether you're celebrating a special occasion or simply looking to indulge in an unforgettable meal, you'll find plenty of options to satisfy your palate and elevate your dining experience in Liechtenstein.

Wine and Spirits: Liechtenstein may be small in size, but it boasts a burgeoning wine industry that produces high-quality wines from vineyards nestled in the Rhine Valley. Visitors can sample a variety of locally produced wines, including crisp whites, fruity rosés, and robust reds, at vineyards and wineries across the principality. In addition to wine, Liechtenstein is also known for its traditional fruit brandies, known as obstler, made from locally grown fruits such as apples, pears, and plums. These artisanal spirits are the perfect way to cap off a delicious meal or toast to a memorable evening in Liechtenstein.

Cafés and Bakeries: No culinary journey through Liechtenstein would be complete without a visit to one of its charming cafés or bakeries, where you can indulge in freshly brewed coffee, decadent pastries, and mouthwatering desserts. Whether you're craving a flaky croissant, a creamy slice of cake, or a warm apple strudel, you'll find plenty of tempting treats to satisfy your sweet tooth in Liechtenstein's cozy cafés and bakeries. Sit back, relax, and savor the moment as you enjoy a taste of Liechtenstein's rich culinary heritage in a warm and welcoming atmosphere.

In summary, dining in Liechtenstein is a culinary adventure that offers a tantalizing blend of tradition, innovation, and local flavors.

Whether you're savoring hearty mountain fare, indulging in fine dining cuisine, or sampling local wines and spirits, you'll find plenty of opportunities to delight your palate and nourish your soul in this charming Alpine principality. So, come hungry, explore with an open mind, and prepare to embark on a culinary journey that will leave you craving more of Liechtenstein's mouthwatering delights.

Chapter 16

Shopping and Markets: Where to Shop

Exploring the shopping scene in Liechtenstein is a delightful adventure, offering travelers a unique blend of traditional craftsmanship, modern boutiques, and bustling markets. From charming village shops to upscale boutiques, the principality has something to offer for every shopper's taste and preference. Join us as we discover the best places to shop in Liechtenstein, where you can find everything from locally made souvenirs to high-end fashion and luxury goods.

Vaduz City Center: The capital city of Vaduz is the premier shopping destination in Liechtenstein, with its charming city center lined with an array of shops, boutiques, and galleries. Here, you'll find everything from trendy fashion boutiques and designer stores to traditional craft shops and souvenir stalls. Take a leisurely stroll along the pedestrian-friendly streets of Vaduz, where you can browse for unique gifts, handmade jewelry, and locally made products to commemorate your visit to Liechtenstein.

Craft Markets: Liechtenstein is known for its rich tradition of craftsmanship, with artisans and craftsmen producing a wide range of high-quality goods, from handmade ceramics and textiles to woodcarvings and glassware. Throughout the year, various craft markets and artisan fairs take place in towns and villages across the principality, offering visitors the opportunity to purchase one-of-a-kind items directly from the makers themselves. These markets are the perfect place to find authentic souvenirs and gifts that capture the essence of Liechtenstein's cultural heritage.

Schloss Vaduz: For a truly unique shopping experience, visit Schloss Vaduz, the ancestral home of the princely family of Liechtenstein. The castle is not only a historic landmark and cultural treasure but also home to a boutique where visitors can purchase exclusive souvenirs, gifts, and memorabilia. From elegant jewelry and fine porcelain to books, postcards, and artwork, the boutique at Schloss Vaduz offers a curated selection of items that reflect the princely heritage and cultural legacy of Liechtenstein.

Galleries and Art Studios: Liechtenstein is home to a vibrant arts and culture scene, with numerous galleries and art studios showcasing the work of local and international artists. Visitors can explore these creative spaces to discover a wide range of artwork, including paintings, sculptures, ceramics, and photography. Many galleries also offer the opportunity to purchase artwork directly from the artists, providing a unique opportunity to acquire original pieces and support the local arts community.

Markets and Flea Markets: Throughout the year, various markets and flea markets take place in Liechtenstein, offering a diverse array of goods, antiques, and treasures waiting to be discovered. From fresh produce and local delicacies to vintage clothing and collectibles, these markets are a treasure trove of hidden gems and unique finds. Whether you're searching for a special souvenir or simply enjoy browsing for bargains, you're sure to find something to pique your interest at one of Liechtenstein's lively markets.

Fashion and Luxury Boutiques: Liechtenstein may be small in size, but it boasts a surprising array of fashion and luxury boutiques catering to discerning shoppers. In Vaduz and other major towns, you'll find boutique shops offering a curated selection of designer clothing, accessories, and luxury goods from renowned international brands. Whether you're in the market for high-end fashion, luxury watches, or upscale home décor, Liechtenstein's boutiques have something to suit every style and taste.

Shopping Centers and Malls: While Liechtenstein may not have large shopping centers or malls like those found in bigger cities, neighboring Switzerland and Austria are home to several shopping centers and outlet malls that are easily accessible from the principality. These modern retail destinations offer a wide range of shops, restaurants, and entertainment options, making them popular destinations for day trips and shopping excursions for visitors to Liechtenstein.

In summary, shopping in Liechtenstein offers a delightful blend of tradition, craftsmanship, and modernity, with a wide range of shops, boutiques, markets, and galleries waiting to be explored. Whether you're searching for unique souvenirs, high-end fashion, or original artwork, you'll find plenty of opportunities to indulge your shopping desires and discover hidden treasures in this charming Alpine principality. So, grab your shopping bags, hit the streets, and prepare to shop 'til you drop as you explore the best places to shop in Liechtenstein.

Chapter 17
Entertainment and Nightlife

As the sun dips below the jagged peaks of the Alps, Liechtenstein transforms into a playground of vibrant entertainment and lively nightlife, offering travelers an array of experiences to unwind and enjoy after a day of exploration. From cozy pubs and chic lounges to cultural events and outdoor concerts, the principality offers something to suit every taste and mood. So, let's delve into the diverse and dynamic world of entertainment and nightlife in Liechtenstein, where the evenings are as enchanting as the days are breathtaking.

Bars and Pubs: Nestled within Liechtenstein's charming towns and villages are an array of inviting bars and cozy pubs, each offering its own unique ambiance and selection of libations. Whether you're seeking a classic pint of beer in a rustic tavern or a handcrafted cocktail in a trendy lounge, you'll find a welcoming spot to relax and unwind after a day of adventure. Strike up a conversation with friendly locals, savor the flavors of local brews, and immerse yourself in the warm and convivial atmosphere of Liechtenstein's bars and pubs.

Live Music: Music has a way of bringing people together, and Liechtenstein's live music scene offers plenty of opportunities to connect with fellow travelers and locals alike. From intimate acoustic performances in cozy cafes to electrifying concerts in bustling venues, there's a diverse range of musical experiences to discover. Whether you're tapping your feet to the rhythms of jazz, rock, or classical melodies, the principality's stages come alive with the sounds of talented musicians from near and far, promising an unforgettable night of entertainment for music lovers of all tastes.

Cultural Events: Dive into Liechtenstein's rich cultural tapestry by immersing yourself in the array of events and festivals that grace the principality's calendar throughout the year. From traditional folk celebrations and art exhibitions to theatrical performances and film screenings, there's always something captivating happening on the cultural front. Explore the depths of Liechtenstein's heritage, mingle with locals, and revel in the creativity and passion that infuse the principality's cultural scene.

Casinos and Gaming: Feeling lucky? Head to one of Liechtenstein's casinos or gaming establishments to test your fortune and indulge in a bit of excitement. Whether you're a seasoned player or a novice looking to try your hand at the tables, the casinos offer an electrifying atmosphere and a chance to win big—or simply enjoy an evening of entertainment and thrills.

Outdoor Activities: For those who prefer their entertainment under the open sky, Liechtenstein offers a wealth of outdoor activities to enjoy after dark. From moonlit hikes and stargazing excursions to nighttime sledding and ice skating, there's no shortage of adventures to embark on once the sun goes down. Soak in the tranquility of the Alpine landscape or revel in the adrenaline of nighttime sports—it's all part of the magic of experiencing Liechtenstein after dark.

Dining Experiences: Dining in Liechtenstein isn't just about satisfying your hunger—it's a culinary journey that engages all the senses. After dark, the principality's restaurants come alive with the aromas of sizzling meats, the clinking of glasses, and the laughter of diners enjoying good food and good company. Whether you're savoring a candlelit dinner in a cozy eatery or indulging in a gourmet feast at a fine dining establishment, the evenings in Liechtenstein are filled with culinary delights that are sure to leave a lasting impression.

In summary, entertainment and nightlife in Liechtenstein offer a rich tapestry of experiences, from cozy pubs and live music venues to cultural events and outdoor adventures. Whether you're seeking a relaxing evening of conversation and cocktails or an adrenaline-fueled night of gaming and excitement, the principality has something to satisfy every traveler's desire for fun and relaxation after dark. So, embrace the magic of Liechtenstein's evenings, and let the principality's vibrant nightlife ignite your sense of adventure and wonder.

Chapter 18
Sports and Recreation: Staying Active in Liechtenstein

Nestled in the heart of the Alps, Liechtenstein offers an abundance of opportunities for outdoor adventure and recreational activities, making it a paradise for travelers who love to stay active and explore the great outdoors. Whether you're seeking adrenaline-pumping thrills or serene moments of relaxation, the principality has something to offer for every fitness level and interest. So, lace up your hiking boots, grab your skis or bike, and join us as we delve into the world of sports and recreation in Liechtenstein, where every day is an opportunity for adventure.

Hiking and Trekking: With its pristine alpine landscapes and network of well-marked trails, Liechtenstein is a hiker's paradise. Whether you're a seasoned trekker or a casual walker, you'll find a variety of routes to suit your skill level and preferences. Embark on a leisurely stroll through lush valleys and meadows, or challenge yourself with a steep ascent to a panoramic mountain summit. Along the way, you'll encounter breathtaking scenery, charming mountain huts, and plenty of opportunities to connect with nature and recharge your spirit.

Cycling and Mountain Biking: Explore Liechtenstein's picturesque countryside on two wheels, pedaling along scenic bike paths and mountain trails that wind through forests, along rivers, and past charming villages. Whether you prefer leisurely rides along flat terrain or heart-pumping descents down rugged mountain trails, there are cycling routes to suit every taste and ability. Bring your own bike or rent one locally, and set off on an unforgettable adventure through the stunning landscapes of Liechtenstein.

Skiing and Snowboarding: When winter blankets the principality in snow, Liechtenstein transforms into a winter wonderland, offering excellent skiing and snowboarding opportunities for enthusiasts of all ages and abilities. Hit the slopes at one of Liechtenstein's two ski resorts, Malbun and Steg, where you'll find a variety of runs catering to beginners, intermediates, and advanced skiers alike. With well-groomed pistes, modern lift systems, and stunning alpine scenery, Liechtenstein's ski resorts provide the perfect setting for a memorable day on the snow.

Snowshoeing and Cross-Country Skiing: For a quieter and more tranquil winter experience, explore Liechtenstein's snow-covered landscapes on snowshoes or cross-country skis. Venture off the beaten path and discover hidden valleys, frozen lakes, and pristine forests as you glide through the winter wonderland at your own pace. With a network of designated trails and routes, as well as rental equipment available at local sports shops, snowshoeing and cross-country skiing offer a wonderful way to immerse yourself in the beauty of Liechtenstein's snowy landscapes.

Rock Climbing and Mountaineering: For those seeking a more vertical challenge, Liechtenstein offers excellent opportunities for rock climbing and mountaineering. Test your skills on the rugged limestone cliffs of the Rätikon range, where you'll find a variety of routes ranging from easy scrambles to challenging multi-pitch climbs. With experienced local guides available to lead expeditions and provide instruction, rock climbing and mountaineering in Liechtenstein offer thrilling experiences for adventurers of all levels.

Water Sports: Despite its landlocked location, Liechtenstein offers plenty of opportunities for water sports enthusiasts to enjoy the great outdoors. Head to the banks of the Rhine River for kayaking, rafting, and stand-up paddleboarding adventures, or explore the tranquil waters of the principality's mountain lakes and reservoirs by canoe or rowboat. Whether you're seeking adrenaline-pumping thrills or moments of serenity on the water, Liechtenstein's waterways provide the perfect playground for aquatic adventures.

Paragliding and Hang Gliding: Soar high above Liechtenstein's stunning landscapes and enjoy bird's-eye views of the principality's mountains, valleys, and villages with a paragliding or hang gliding adventure. Experienced pilots and tandem flights are available for those looking to experience the thrill of free flight, while beginners can take lessons to learn the basics and embark on their own soaring adventures. With its clear skies, favorable wind conditions, and breathtaking scenery, Liechtenstein offers an unforgettable playground for aerial adventurers.

Wellness and Relaxation: After a day of outdoor adventure, unwind and rejuvenate your body and mind with a visit to one of Liechtenstein's wellness centers or spas. Treat yourself to a soothing massage, relax in a steam bath or sauna, or take a refreshing dip in a heated indoor pool. With a variety of wellness facilities and treatments available, you'll find plenty of opportunities to pamper yourself and indulge in some well-deserved relaxation during your stay in Liechtenstein.

In summary, sports and recreation in Liechtenstein offer a wealth of opportunities for outdoor adventure, adrenaline-pumping thrills, and moments of relaxation and rejuvenation. Whether you're hiking through pristine mountain landscapes, carving turns on the ski slopes, or soaring high above the alpine peaks, the principality's diverse landscapes and natural beauty provide the perfect backdrop for unforgettable experiences. So, pack your gear, embrace your sense of adventure, and prepare to explore the great outdoors in Liechtenstein—a playground for active travelers seeking excitement, serenity, and everything in between.

Chapter 19
Volunteering and Community Engagement

Beyond its stunning landscapes and rich cultural heritage, Liechtenstein is a place where travelers can immerse themselves in meaningful experiences by giving back to the local community through volunteering and community engagement initiatives. Whether you're passionate about environmental conservation, social welfare, or cultural preservation, there are countless opportunities to make a positive impact and connect with locals while traveling in Liechtenstein. Join us as we explore the rewarding world of volunteering and community engagement in this charming Alpine principality, where every act of kindness helps to strengthen the bonds of community and foster a spirit of goodwill.

Environmental Conservation: Liechtenstein is blessed with pristine natural landscapes, from its lush valleys and meadows to its rugged mountain peaks. Environmental conservation efforts play a crucial role in preserving these precious habitats and protecting the biodiversity of the principality. Travelers interested in conservation can participate in volunteer programs focused on habitat restoration, wildlife monitoring, and sustainable land management. Whether you're planting trees, cleaning up litter, or conducting ecological surveys, volunteering for environmental conservation projects allows you to contribute to the long-term health and vitality of Liechtenstein's ecosystems.

Social Welfare: In addition to its natural beauty, Liechtenstein is also home to vibrant communities where residents support one another through various social welfare initiatives. Travelers interested in social welfare can volunteer their time and skills to support local organizations and charities that provide assistance to vulnerable populations, such as the elderly, refugees, and individuals experiencing homelessness. Whether you're helping to serve meals at a soup kitchen, tutoring children in need, or organizing fundraising events, volunteering for social welfare projects allows you to make a meaningful difference in the lives of others and foster a sense of compassion and empathy within the community.

Cultural Preservation: Liechtenstein has a rich cultural heritage that is celebrated and cherished by its residents, who take pride in preserving their traditions and customs for future generations. Travelers interested in cultural preservation can volunteer for initiatives that promote and safeguard the principality's cultural heritage, such as museum docent programs, historical preservation projects, and cultural events and festivals. Whether you're leading guided tours of historic sites, assisting with artifact conservation, or participating in traditional craft workshops, volunteering for cultural preservation projects allows you to deepen your appreciation for Liechtenstein's heritage and contribute to its ongoing legacy.

Community Events and Festivals: Liechtenstein's communities come together throughout the year to celebrate a variety of cultural, religious, and seasonal festivals and events. Travelers interested in community engagement can volunteer to help organize and support these gatherings, whether it's assisting with event planning and logistics, coordinating activities and entertainment, or helping with setup and cleanup. Volunteering for community events and festivals allows you to connect with locals, experience the joy and camaraderie of celebration, and contribute to the vibrant tapestry of life in Liechtenstein.

Language Exchange and Cultural Exchange: One of the best ways to engage with the local community in Liechtenstein is through language exchange and cultural exchange programs. Travelers interested in language learning can volunteer to teach their native language to locals while learning German or one of Liechtenstein's other official languages in return. Similarly, cultural exchange programs offer opportunities to share your own cultural traditions and customs with locals while immersing yourself in Liechtenstein's rich cultural heritage.

These exchanges foster cross-cultural understanding and friendship, enriching both the traveler's experience and the local community.

Nonprofit Organizations and NGOs: Liechtenstein is home to a variety of nonprofit organizations and non-governmental organizations (NGOs) that work on a wide range of social, environmental, and cultural issues. Travelers interested in volunteering can reach out to these organizations to inquire about volunteer opportunities and get involved in projects that align with their interests and skills. Whether it's supporting youth development programs, advocating for human rights, or promoting sustainable development initiatives, volunteering for nonprofit organizations and NGOs allows travelers to contribute to positive change and make a difference in Liechtenstein and beyond.

In summary, volunteering and community engagement offer travelers a unique opportunity to connect with locals, make a positive impact, and deepen their understanding of the culture and values of Liechtenstein. Whether you're passionate about environmental conservation, social welfare, cultural preservation, or community development, there are countless ways to get involved and give back while traveling in this charming Alpine principality. So, roll up your sleeves, open your heart, and prepare to make a difference in the lives of others as you embark on a journey of service and solidarity in Liechtenstein.

Chapter 20
Socializing and Making Friends

Traveling to a new country is not just about exploring its sights and attractions—it's also about connecting with the people who call it home and forging meaningful friendships that transcend borders. In Liechtenstein, a small but welcoming Alpine principality, socializing and making friends is an integral part of the travel experience, offering visitors the opportunity to connect with locals, immerse themselves in the culture, and create memories that last a lifetime. So, whether you're sipping coffee in a cozy café, joining a hiking group in the mountains, or attending a cultural event in the capital city, there are countless ways to socialize and make friends in Liechtenstein.

Embrace the Café Culture: In Liechtenstein, socializing often revolves around the café culture, where locals gather to enjoy coffee, conversation, and good company. Take a seat at a sidewalk café or cozy coffeehouse, order your favorite brew, and strike up a conversation with fellow patrons or the friendly barista. Whether you're discussing the weather, sharing travel stories, or swapping recommendations for the best local sights and experiences, cafés provide the perfect setting for casual socializing and making new friends in Liechtenstein.

Join Group Activities and Events: One of the best ways to meet people and make friends in Liechtenstein is by joining group activities and events that align with your interests and hobbies. Whether you're passionate about hiking, cycling, photography, or art, there are plenty of clubs, meetups, and organized events where you can connect with like-minded individuals and enjoy shared experiences. Keep an eye out for flyers, posters, and online forums advertising upcoming activities and events, and don't be afraid to step out of your comfort zone and join in the fun.

Attend Cultural Events and Festivals: Liechtenstein's cultural calendar is filled with a variety of events and festivals that offer excellent opportunities for socializing and making friends. Whether you're attending a concert, art exhibition, or traditional folk festival, these gatherings provide a vibrant and festive atmosphere where locals and visitors come together to celebrate and connect. Strike up conversations with fellow attendees, participate in activities and performances, and immerse yourself in the cultural traditions and customs of Liechtenstein.

Explore Outdoor Recreation: The stunning landscapes of Liechtenstein provide the perfect backdrop for outdoor recreation and adventure, offering travelers the chance to connect with nature and with each other. Whether you're hiking through lush forests, skiing down snow-covered slopes, or paddling along tranquil rivers, outdoor activities provide opportunities for socializing and bonding with fellow outdoor enthusiasts. Join guided tours, group excursions, or outdoor clubs to meet new people and share unforgettable experiences in the great outdoors.

Learn the Language: Language is the key to communication and connection, and learning a few words of the local language can go a long way in making friends in Liechtenstein. While German is the official language of the principality, many residents also speak English and other languages, so don't be shy about practicing your language skills and engaging in conversations with locals. Sign up for language classes, attend language exchange meetups, or simply strike up conversations with locals in cafes and shops to improve your language proficiency and build meaningful connections.

Volunteer and Give Back: Volunteering is not only a great way to give back to the community, but it's also an excellent way to meet new people and make friends who share your values and interests. Whether you're participating in environmental clean-up projects, assisting at local charities, or volunteering at cultural events, volunteering provides opportunities to connect with locals, work towards common goals, and make a positive impact in the community. So, roll up your sleeves, get involved, and discover the rewards of giving back while making new friends in Liechtenstein.

Be Open and Approachable: Above all, be open, approachable, and willing to engage with others while traveling in Liechtenstein. Smile, make eye contact, and show genuine interest in the people you meet, whether they're locals or fellow travelers. Be respectful of cultural differences, listen actively, and be willing to share your own experiences and stories. By embracing a positive and open-minded attitude, you'll create opportunities for meaningful connections and friendships to flourish in Liechtenstein.

In summary, socializing and making friends in Liechtenstein is a rewarding and enriching experience that offers travelers the opportunity to connect with locals, immerse themselves in the culture, and create lasting memories. Whether you're enjoying coffee in a café, exploring the outdoors, attending cultural events, or volunteering in the community, there are countless ways to meet new people and forge meaningful connections in this charming Alpine principality. So, step out of your comfort zone, embrace new experiences, and get ready to make friends and create unforgettable moments in Liechtenstein.

Chapter 21
Religious Practices and Places of Worship

Religion plays a significant role in the cultural fabric of Liechtenstein, a small Alpine principality with a rich religious heritage that spans centuries. From ancient churches and historic monasteries to vibrant religious festivals and traditions, Liechtenstein offers travelers a fascinating glimpse into the spiritual life of its people. Whether you're a devout believer seeking to explore sacred sites or simply curious about the religious practices of the principality, there's much to discover and appreciate in Liechtenstein's religious landscape.

Christianity in Liechtenstein: The predominant religion in Liechtenstein is Christianity, with the Roman Catholic Church being the largest Christian denomination in the principality. The Catholic faith has deep historical roots in Liechtenstein, dating back to the early Middle Ages when Christianity was first introduced to the region by missionaries and monks. Today, the Catholic Church remains a central pillar of religious life in Liechtenstein, with a network of churches, chapels, and monasteries serving the spiritual needs of the faithful.

Places of Worship: Liechtenstein is home to a variety of churches, chapels, and religious sites that reflect the diversity of its religious heritage. In the capital city of Vaduz and throughout the principality's towns and villages, visitors will find a wealth of historic churches and chapels dating back to medieval times, each with its own unique architecture, artwork, and religious significance. From the iconic Vaduz Cathedral, with its striking twin towers and Baroque interior, to the quaint village churches nestled amid picturesque landscapes, Liechtenstein's places of worship offer visitors a glimpse into the spiritual heart of the principality.

Religious Festivals and Traditions: Throughout the year, Liechtenstein celebrates a variety of religious festivals and traditions that hold special significance for its residents. From Christmas and Easter to Corpus Christi and Assumption Day, these festivals are marked by religious observances, processions, and ceremonies that reflect the deep faith and cultural traditions of the principality. Visitors are often welcomed to participate in these celebrations, providing an opportunity to experience the rich tapestry of religious life in Liechtenstein and witness the strong sense of community and devotion that characterizes its religious festivals.

Monasteries and Religious Communities: Liechtenstein is also home to several monasteries and religious communities that play a vital role in the spiritual and cultural life of the principality. From the Benedictine Abbey of Marienberg, perched atop a hill overlooking the Rhine Valley, to the Capuchin Monastery in Triesen, these religious institutions have long been centers of prayer, contemplation, and hospitality. Visitors can often participate in guided tours, attend religious services, or even stay overnight as guests of the monastic communities, providing a unique opportunity to experience the tranquility and spiritual heritage of Liechtenstein's monastic tradition.

Interfaith Dialogue and Tolerance: Despite its predominantly Christian population, Liechtenstein is a place where religious diversity is respected and valued. While the Catholic Church remains the largest religious denomination, the principality is also home to small communities of Protestants, Muslims, Jews, and other faith traditions. Interfaith dialogue and cooperation are encouraged, with various initiatives and organizations promoting mutual understanding, respect, and tolerance among different religious communities. Visitors to Liechtenstein will find a welcoming and inclusive atmosphere where people of all faiths are invited to explore and engage with the religious diversity of the principality.

Practical Considerations: When visiting religious sites in Liechtenstein, it's important to respect local customs and traditions. Modest attire is often expected when entering churches and other places of worship, with shoulders and knees typically covered out of respect for religious sensibilities. Visitors should also be mindful of any religious services or ceremonies taking place and avoid disrupting worshippers or taking photographs without permission. By showing respect for the sacredness of these sites and the religious practices of the local community, visitors can ensure a meaningful and respectful experience when exploring Liechtenstein's religious heritage.

In summary, religious practices and places of worship in Liechtenstein offer travelers a window into the spiritual life and cultural traditions of the principality. Whether you're exploring historic churches, participating in religious festivals, or engaging in interfaith dialogue, there are countless opportunities to deepen your understanding of Liechtenstein's religious heritage and connect with its people on a spiritual level. So, whether you're a devout believer or simply curious about the religious traditions of the principality, be sure to explore the rich tapestry of religious life in Liechtenstein during your travels.

Chapter 22
Legal Matters: Understanding the Law

As a traveler exploring the picturesque landscapes and charming towns of Liechtenstein, it's important to have a basic understanding of the legal framework that governs the principality. While Liechtenstein is known for its safety, security, and rule of law, there are still important legal matters that travelers should be aware of to ensure a smooth and enjoyable experience during their visit. From immigration and customs regulations to local laws and cultural norms, this chapter aims to provide travelers with the essential information they need to navigate legal matters in Liechtenstein responsibly and respectfully.

Immigration and Entry Requirements: Travelers planning to visit Liechtenstein should be aware of the immigration and entry requirements that apply to their specific situation. Liechtenstein is part of the Schengen Area, which allows for visa-free travel for citizens of certain countries for short stays. However, travelers from non-Schengen countries may need to obtain a visa before entering Liechtenstein, depending on their nationality and the purpose of their visit. It's essential to check the latest visa requirements and regulations before traveling to Liechtenstein to ensure compliance with immigration laws.

Customs Regulations: Upon entering Liechtenstein, travelers are subject to customs regulations that govern the importation of goods into the principality. While Liechtenstein is not a member of the European Union (EU), it is part of the European Economic Area (EEA), which means that many EU customs regulations apply. Travelers should be aware of duty-free allowances, restrictions on certain goods (such as alcohol, tobacco, and firearms), and requirements for declaring items of value upon entry. Failure to comply with customs regulations can result in fines or confiscation of goods, so it's important to familiarize yourself with the rules before crossing the border into Liechtenstein.

Local Laws and Regulations: While visiting Liechtenstein, travelers are expected to abide by the local laws and regulations that govern behavior and conduct within the principality. While Liechtenstein is known for its safety and low crime rate, travelers should still exercise common sense and caution to avoid running afoul of the law. Some important legal considerations for travelers include:

- Traffic laws: Liechtenstein has strict traffic laws governing speed limits, seat belt use, and driving under the influence of alcohol or drugs. Travelers should familiarize themselves with local traffic regulations and adhere to them when driving in the principality.
- Alcohol and drug laws: The legal drinking age in Liechtenstein is 16 for beer and wine and 18 for spirits. Driving under the influence of alcohol or drugs is strictly prohibited and can result in severe penalties, including fines, license suspension, and imprisonment.
- Public behavior: Public drunkenness, disorderly conduct, and acts of vandalism are not tolerated in Liechtenstein and can result in fines or other legal consequences. Travelers should respect local customs and cultural norms and conduct themselves in a respectful and responsible manner at all times.

Cultural Sensitivity and Respect: In addition to legal considerations, travelers should also be mindful of cultural sensitivities and norms when visiting Liechtenstein. The principality has a strong sense of tradition and values, and travelers should respect local customs, traditions, and religious practices. This includes dressing modestly when visiting religious sites, refraining from loud or disruptive behavior in public spaces, and asking for permission before taking photographs of individuals or cultural events. By showing respect for the customs and traditions of Liechtenstein, travelers can ensure a positive and enriching experience during their visit.

Emergency Services and Assistance: In the event of an emergency or legal issue during your visit to Liechtenstein, travelers can rely on the principality's well-developed system of emergency services and assistance. The national emergency number in Liechtenstein is 112, which can be dialed for police, fire, or medical assistance. Additionally, travelers can seek assistance from their embassy or consulate in Liechtenstein for consular services, legal advice, or assistance with emergency situations.

In summary, understanding the legal matters and regulations that apply to travelers in Liechtenstein is essential for ensuring a safe, enjoyable, and responsible visit to the principality. By familiarizing yourself with immigration requirements, customs regulations, local laws, and cultural norms, you can navigate legal matters in Liechtenstein with confidence and respect for the laws and customs of the principality. So, whether you're exploring the historic sites of Vaduz, hiking in the mountains, or attending a cultural event, be sure to stay informed and abide by the legal requirements and expectations of Liechtenstein during your travels.

Chapter 23
Taxes and Financial Planning

As you embark on your journey to explore the scenic beauty and cultural richness of Liechtenstein, it's essential to have a basic understanding of the principality's tax system and financial regulations. Whether you're planning a short-term visit or considering a more permanent move to Liechtenstein, being informed about taxes and financial planning can help you make sound decisions and navigate your financial affairs responsibly. In this chapter, we'll delve into the key aspects of taxes, banking, and financial planning in Liechtenstein, providing you with the knowledge you need to manage your finances effectively during your stay in the principality.

Tax System Overview: Liechtenstein operates under a territorial tax system, which means that taxes are levied only on income and assets earned or held within the principality's borders. The tax system in Liechtenstein is characterized by low tax rates and favorable tax conditions for individuals and businesses, making it an attractive destination for investors and high-net-worth individuals. The main types of taxes in Liechtenstein include income tax, wealth tax, inheritance tax, and value-added tax (VAT), each with its own set of regulations and exemptions.

Income Tax: Individual income tax in Liechtenstein is levied on a progressive scale, with tax rates ranging from 1.2% to 8.0% based on income levels. Residents of Liechtenstein are subject to taxation on their worldwide income, while non-residents are only taxed on income earned within the principality's borders. Liechtenstein also offers various tax incentives and deductions for certain types of income, such as investment income, capital gains, and contributions to pension schemes, to encourage investment and economic growth.

Wealth Tax: Liechtenstein imposes a wealth tax on the worldwide assets of residents, including real estate, financial assets, and other forms of wealth. The wealth tax rate varies depending on the value of the individual's assets and ranges from 0.06% to 0.8%. Non-residents are not subject to wealth tax on assets held outside of Liechtenstein, but they may be subject to taxation on assets located within the principality.

Inheritance and Gift Tax: Liechtenstein does not levy inheritance or gift tax on transfers of wealth between family members, making it an attractive jurisdiction for estate planning and wealth transfer. However, certain conditions and restrictions may apply, so it's essential to seek professional advice when planning for inheritance or making gifts to ensure compliance with the relevant regulations.

Value-Added Tax (VAT): Liechtenstein imposes a standard VAT rate of 7.7% on the sale of goods and services within its borders. Certain goods and services may be exempt from VAT or subject to reduced rates, depending on their nature and usage. Visitors to Liechtenstein can claim VAT refunds on eligible purchases made during their stay by following the procedures outlined by the principality's tax authorities.

Banking and Financial Services: Liechtenstein is renowned for its robust banking and financial services sector, which offers a wide range of products and services to domestic and international clients. The principality's banks are known for their stability, discretion, and adherence to strict banking regulations, making them a preferred destination for individuals and businesses seeking secure and reliable banking solutions. Liechtenstein is also a global leader in wealth management and private banking, offering tailored financial solutions to high-net-worth individuals and families around the world.

Financial Planning Considerations: Whether you're a short-term visitor or considering a more permanent move to Liechtenstein, careful financial planning is essential for managing your finances effectively and achieving your financial goals. Considerations such as budgeting, saving, investing, and retirement planning should be taken into account to ensure long-term financial security and stability. Consulting with financial advisors or wealth managers with expertise in Liechtenstein's tax and financial regulations can help you develop a personalized financial plan that aligns with your needs and objectives.

Compliance and Reporting Obligations: Finally, it's important to be aware of your compliance and reporting obligations under Liechtenstein's tax and financial regulations. Residents and taxpayers in Liechtenstein are required to file annual tax returns and comply with reporting requirements for foreign assets and income. Failure to meet these obligations can result in penalties, fines, or other legal consequences, so it's crucial to stay informed and fulfill your tax and reporting obligations in a timely and accurate manner.

In summary, understanding taxes and financial planning in Liechtenstein is essential for managing your finances effectively and responsibly during your stay in the principality. Whether you're a visitor, investor, or resident, being informed about the tax system, banking regulations, and financial planning considerations can help you make informed decisions and navigate your financial affairs with confidence. So, whether you're exploring the cultural treasures of Vaduz, enjoying outdoor adventures in the mountains, or planning for your future in Liechtenstein, be sure to consider the tax and financial implications of your activities and seek professional advice when needed.

Chapter 24
Climate and Weather: What to Expect

As you prepare for your journey to Liechtenstein, it's essential to familiarize yourself with the climate and weather conditions you can expect during your visit. Nestled in the heart of the Alps, Liechtenstein experiences a continental climate characterized by four distinct seasons, each offering its own unique charm and opportunities for exploration. From the snow-capped peaks of winter to the blooming meadows of spring, the sunny days of summer, and the vibrant foliage of autumn, Liechtenstein's climate promises a diverse and captivating experience for travelers year-round.

Winter (December - February): Winter in Liechtenstein brings a magical transformation to the principality's landscapes, as snow blankets the mountains and valleys, creating a picturesque winter wonderland. Temperatures during the winter months can vary widely, with average daytime temperatures ranging from 0°C to 5°C (32°F to 41°F) in the lowlands and dropping below freezing in the higher elevations. Skiing, snowboarding, and other winter sports are popular activities during this time, with numerous ski resorts offering excellent conditions for outdoor enthusiasts of all levels.

Spring (March - May): As the snow begins to melt and the days grow longer, Liechtenstein emerges from its winter slumber with the vibrant colors and fragrant blooms of spring. Temperatures gradually warm up during the spring months, with average daytime temperatures ranging from 8°C to 15°C (46°F to 59°F). Spring is an ideal time to explore Liechtenstein's scenic hiking trails, bike paths, and nature reserves, as the countryside comes alive with fresh greenery and blossoming flowers.

Summer (June - August): Summer in Liechtenstein is a time of warmth, sunshine, and outdoor adventure, as the principality enjoys long days and pleasant temperatures. Average daytime temperatures during the summer months range from 20°C to 25°C (68°F to 77°F), making it perfect for hiking, cycling, swimming, and exploring the great outdoors. From picnicking in scenic parks to attending outdoor concerts and festivals, there's no shortage of activities to enjoy during the summer in Liechtenstein.

Autumn (September - November): As summer fades into autumn, Liechtenstein's landscapes undergo a breathtaking transformation, as the leaves turn vibrant shades of red, orange, and gold. Average daytime temperatures during the autumn months range from 10°C to 15°C (50°F to 59°F), creating ideal conditions for hiking, leaf-peeping, and enjoying the natural beauty of the principality. Autumn is also a time of harvest festivals and culinary delights, as local farmers celebrate the bounty of the season with traditional dishes and culinary events.

Microclimates and Regional Variations: While Liechtenstein has a relatively small geographical area, it boasts diverse microclimates and regional variations due to its mountainous terrain and proximity to the Rhine Valley. The northern region of Liechtenstein, bordering Switzerland, tends to be slightly warmer and drier than the southern region, which is more influenced by the Alps. Additionally, elevation plays a significant role in determining local weather conditions, with higher elevations experiencing cooler temperatures and more precipitation than lower-lying areas.

Weather Patterns and Forecasting: Liechtenstein's weather can be unpredictable at times, with rapid changes in weather patterns and localized microclimates. It's essential to stay informed about current weather conditions and forecasts, especially if you plan to engage in outdoor activities or travel to different regions of the principality. Local weather forecasts are readily available through online weather websites, mobile apps, and traditional media outlets, providing up-to-date information on temperature, precipitation, wind, and other relevant weather parameters.

Packing Tips: When preparing for your trip to Liechtenstein, it's important to pack accordingly based on the season and anticipated weather conditions. In the winter, be sure to bring warm layers, waterproof outerwear, and sturdy footwear for outdoor activities in the snow. In the summer, lightweight clothing, sunscreen, sunglasses, and a hat are essential for staying comfortable in the warm weather. Regardless of the season, it's always a good idea to pack a versatile wardrobe that can adapt to changing weather conditions and outdoor adventures.

In summary, Liechtenstein's climate offers travelers a diverse and captivating experience throughout the year, with each season bringing its own unique beauty and opportunities for exploration. Whether you're skiing in the winter, hiking in the spring, swimming in the summer, or leaf-peeping in the autumn, Liechtenstein's climate promises an unforgettable journey filled with natural wonders and outdoor adventures. So, pack your bags, dress for the weather, and get ready to immerse yourself in the breathtaking landscapes and ever-changing weather of Liechtenstein during your travels.

Chapter 25
Safety and Emergency Services

Ensuring your safety and well-being is paramount when traveling to any destination, and Liechtenstein, with its reputation for safety, is no exception. While the principality is known for its low crime rate, stunning landscapes, and welcoming atmosphere, it's still essential for travelers to be informed about safety precautions, emergency services, and local regulations to ensure a smooth and worry-free experience during their visit. In this chapter, we'll explore the various aspects of safety in Liechtenstein, including crime, health, natural disasters, and emergency services, providing you with the knowledge and resources you need to stay safe and secure throughout your travels.

Crime and Personal Safety: Liechtenstein is widely regarded as one of the safest countries in the world, with low crime rates and a strong emphasis on public safety and security. Violent crime is extremely rare, and travelers can generally feel safe exploring the principality's towns, villages, and countryside both day and night. However, as with any destination, it's essential to exercise common sense and take basic precautions to ensure your personal safety. These include:

- Keeping your belongings secure and valuables out of sight, especially in crowded tourist areas.
- Avoiding isolated or poorly lit areas, particularly at night.
- Being vigilant of your surroundings and alert to any suspicious behavior or activities.
- Following local laws and regulations, including traffic laws and restrictions on alcohol consumption.

Health and Medical Services: Liechtenstein boasts a modern and well-developed healthcare system that provides high-quality medical care to residents and visitors alike. The principality is home to hospitals, clinics, and medical facilities equipped with state-of-the-art technology and staffed by skilled healthcare professionals. In the event of a medical emergency or illness during your visit, you can rely on the following resources:

- Emergency medical services: The national emergency number in Liechtenstein is 112, which can be dialed for medical assistance in case of emergencies. Trained paramedics and emergency medical personnel are available to provide immediate assistance and transport to the nearest hospital or medical facility.
- Hospitals and clinics: Liechtenstein has several hospitals and medical clinics located throughout the principality, offering a range of medical services, including emergency care, surgery, and specialty treatments. Vaduz Hospital, located in the capital city, is the main medical facility in Liechtenstein and provides comprehensive healthcare services to residents and visitors.
- Pharmacies: Pharmacies (Apotheken) in Liechtenstein dispense prescription medications and over-the-counter drugs, as well as provide advice and information on healthcare and medication. Most pharmacies operate during regular business hours, with some offering after-hours and emergency services for urgent medical needs.

Natural Disasters and Emergency Preparedness: While Liechtenstein is not prone to major natural disasters such as earthquakes or hurricanes, travelers should still be prepared for potential emergencies and adverse weather conditions. Common natural hazards in Liechtenstein include heavy snowfall, avalanches, and flooding, particularly in mountainous areas. To stay safe during your visit, consider the following tips:

- Check weather forecasts and warnings before engaging in outdoor activities, especially in mountainous regions.
- Follow local authorities' advice and instructions in the event of severe weather or natural disasters.
- Carry essential supplies and emergency equipment, such as food, water, blankets, and a first-aid kit, when traveling in remote or isolated areas.
- Stay informed about potential hazards and emergency procedures, including evacuation routes and shelter locations.

Emergency Services and Assistance: In the event of an emergency or crisis during your visit to Liechtenstein, you can rely on the principality's well-developed system of emergency services and assistance. In addition to medical emergencies, travelers can contact emergency services for assistance with accidents, incidents, or other urgent situations. Important contact numbers and resources include:

- Police: 117 (for non-emergency police assistance)
- Fire and Rescue Services: 118
- Mountain Rescue Services: +423 230 22 22
- Poison Control Center: +41 44 251 51 51

Travel Insurance and Documentation: Before traveling to Liechtenstein, it's advisable to obtain comprehensive travel insurance that includes coverage for medical emergencies, trip cancellation, and other unforeseen events. Travel insurance provides financial protection and peace of mind in the event of unexpected expenses or emergencies during your trip. Additionally, make sure to carry important documents such as your passport, identification, and medical insurance information with you at all times, and keep copies in a safe and secure location.

In summary, safety and emergency services in Liechtenstein are designed to ensure the well-being and security of residents and visitors alike. By staying informed, exercising caution, and being prepared for potential emergencies, travelers can enjoy a safe and memorable experience in this enchanting Alpine principality. So, whether you're exploring historic landmarks, hiking in the mountains, or sampling local cuisine, take the necessary precautions to stay safe and secure during your travels in Liechtenstein.

Chapter 26
Pet Ownership: Guidelines and Regulations

For many travelers, pets are cherished members of the family, and the thought of leaving them behind when embarking on a journey can be daunting. If you're considering bringing your furry friend along on your visit to Liechtenstein, it's essential to be aware of the guidelines and regulations governing pet ownership in the principality. From entry requirements and transportation regulations to pet-friendly accommodations and outdoor activities, this chapter aims to provide you with the information you need to ensure a smooth and enjoyable experience for both you and your pet during your travels in Liechtenstein.

Pet Entry Requirements: Before traveling to Liechtenstein with your pet, it's important to familiarize yourself with the entry requirements and regulations that apply to bringing animals into the principality. While Liechtenstein is part of the Schengen Area, which allows for the free movement of pets within certain countries, there are still specific requirements that must be met to ensure the health and safety of both pets and residents. These may include:

- Microchipping: Pets entering Liechtenstein are required to be microchipped for identification purposes. The microchip should comply with ISO standards and be compatible with international scanners.
- Vaccinations: Dogs, cats, and ferrets entering Liechtenstein must be vaccinated against rabies, with the vaccination administered at least 21 days before travel. Proof of rabies vaccination, in the form of a pet passport or official veterinary certificate, is required for entry.
- Health Certificate: In addition to rabies vaccination, pets

may need to obtain a health certificate from a licensed veterinarian issued within a specified timeframe before travel. The health certificate should certify that the pet is in good health and free from contagious diseases.
- Additional Requirements: Depending on the type of animal and its country of origin, additional requirements such as blood tests, parasite treatments, or import permits may be necessary. It's essential to check the latest entry requirements and regulations for pets traveling to Liechtenstein to ensure compliance with all necessary procedures.

Transportation and Accommodations: Traveling with pets to Liechtenstein requires careful planning and consideration, particularly when it comes to transportation and accommodations. When traveling by air, it's essential to research airline pet policies and regulations regarding pet carriers, crate sizes, and in-cabin or cargo transportation options. Many airlines offer pet-friendly services and amenities to ensure the comfort and safety of traveling pets, but advance booking and preparation are recommended to secure space for your pet on the flight.

Similarly, when selecting accommodations in Liechtenstein, it's important to choose pet-friendly hotels, guesthouses, or vacation rentals that welcome pets and provide suitable accommodations for both you and your furry companion. Many hotels and accommodations in Liechtenstein offer pet-friendly rooms or facilities, but it's always best to confirm availability and any additional fees or restrictions before booking your stay.

Outdoor Activities and Recreation: Liechtenstein's stunning natural landscapes and outdoor attractions offer countless opportunities for pet owners to explore and enjoy outdoor adventures with their furry friends. From scenic hikes and nature trails to lakeside picnics and mountain excursions, there's no shortage of pet-friendly activities to experience in the principality. Some popular outdoor destinations and activities for pets and their owners in Liechtenstein include:

- Hiking trails: Liechtenstein boasts a network of well-maintained hiking trails that wind through picturesque valleys, forests, and mountains, offering scenic views and fresh mountain air for hikers and their pets to enjoy.
- Parks and green spaces: Vaduz, the capital city of Liechtenstein, is home to several parks and green spaces where pets are welcome to roam and play off-leash. These include the Vaduzer Stadtpark, a beautiful park with walking paths, benches, and open spaces for pets to explore.
- Lakes and rivers: Liechtenstein's pristine lakes and rivers provide opportunities for water-based activities such as swimming, boating, and fishing, with many areas accessible to pets and their owners for leisurely strolls or water play.
- Pet-friendly attractions: Many tourist attractions and cultural sites in Liechtenstein welcome pets and their owners, allowing them to explore historic landmarks, museums, and exhibitions together. Some popular pet-friendly attractions include Vaduz Castle, the Liechtenstein National Museum, and the Triesenberg Church.

Local Regulations and Etiquette: While exploring Liechtenstein with your pet, it's important to be mindful of local regulations, etiquette, and cultural norms regarding pet ownership and behavior. Pets should be kept on a leash in public places, and owners are responsible for cleaning up after their pets and disposing of waste properly. Additionally, it's essential to respect private property and the rights of other residents and visitors when traveling with pets, ensuring that your pet's presence does not disturb or inconvenience others.

In summary, traveling to Liechtenstein with your pet can be a rewarding and memorable experience, provided you take the necessary precautions and considerations to ensure the health, safety, and well-being of your furry companion. By familiarizing yourself with entry requirements, transportation options, pet-friendly accommodations, and local regulations, you can enjoy a hassle-free and enjoyable journey with your pet in this charming Alpine principality. So, pack your pet's favorite toys, leash, and travel essentials, and get ready to embark on an adventure together in pet-friendly Liechtenstein.

Chapter 27
Day Trips and Excursions: Exploring the Region

While Liechtenstein offers a wealth of attractions and activities within its borders, the principality's central location in Europe makes it an ideal base for exploring the surrounding region. From charming alpine villages and historic cities to stunning natural landscapes and cultural treasures, there are countless day trips and excursions to enjoy just a short distance from Liechtenstein. Whether you're interested in history, art, outdoor adventures, or culinary delights, the region surrounding Liechtenstein offers something for every traveler to discover and explore.

Vaduz to Feldkirch, Austria: Just a short drive from Vaduz, the capital of Liechtenstein, lies the picturesque town of Feldkirch in neighboring Austria. This historic town is known for its well-preserved medieval architecture, charming cobblestone streets, and vibrant cultural scene. Visitors can explore the medieval town center, visit the imposing Schattenburg Castle, or enjoy panoramic views of the surrounding mountains from the nearby observation tower. Feldkirch also boasts a thriving culinary scene, with traditional Austrian restaurants, cafes, and wine bars offering delicious regional specialties and local wines.

Vaduz to Chur, Switzerland: For a scenic day trip through the Swiss Alps, consider visiting the charming city of Chur, the oldest city in Switzerland. Located just a short drive from Vaduz, Chur is known for its well-preserved old town, historic landmarks, and vibrant cultural scene. Visitors can explore the winding alleys and medieval buildings of the old town, visit the impressive Chur Cathedral, or take a leisurely stroll along the banks of the Rhine River. Chur is also a gateway to the nearby Swiss Alps, with opportunities for hiking, skiing, and outdoor adventures in the surrounding mountains.

Vaduz to Lake Constance: Situated on the border of Germany, Austria, and Switzerland, Lake Constance is one of the largest and most picturesque lakes in Europe. A day trip from Vaduz to Lake Constance offers visitors the opportunity to explore charming lakeside towns, visit historic castles and museums, and enjoy a variety of water-based activities. Highlights of a visit to Lake Constance include the medieval town of Konstanz, the flower island of Mainau, and the charming village of Meersburg. Visitors can also take boat tours of the lake, go swimming or sailing, or simply relax on the shores and enjoy the stunning views.

Vaduz to Appenzell, Switzerland: Nestled in the rolling hills of eastern Switzerland, the town of Appenzell is renowned for its traditional Swiss architecture, colorful facades, and vibrant folk culture. A day trip from Vaduz to Appenzell offers visitors the chance to explore the town's historic center, visit the iconic Appenzell Museum, and sample local specialties such as Appenzeller cheese and traditional Swiss chocolate. Visitors can also hike in the surrounding hills and mountains, take scenic drives through the Appenzell countryside, or attend one of the town's famous folk festivals and events.

Vaduz to Liechtenstein Trail: For those looking to explore closer to home, the Liechtenstein Trail offers a scenic hiking route that spans the length of the principality, passing through picturesque villages, rolling hills, and lush forests along the way. The trail is divided into 14 stages, each offering stunning views and opportunities to discover the natural beauty and cultural heritage of Liechtenstein. Hikers can explore historic landmarks, visit local attractions, and enjoy outdoor activities such as picnicking, birdwatching, and wildlife spotting along the trail.

Practical Tips for Day Trips: When planning day trips and excursions from Liechtenstein, there are a few practical tips to keep in mind to ensure a smooth and enjoyable experience:

- Check transportation options: Research transportation options such as trains, buses, and car rentals to reach your desired destination. Consider factors such as travel time, cost, and convenience when choosing the best mode of transportation for your day trip.
- Plan your itinerary: Take time to research and plan your itinerary, including attractions, activities, and dining options. Consider any time constraints, opening hours, or seasonal closures when scheduling your day trip activities.
- Pack essentials: Be sure to pack essentials such as water, snacks, sunscreen, comfortable footwear, and weather-appropriate clothing for your day trip. Consider any specific gear or equipment you may need for outdoor activities such as hiking or swimming.
- Stay informed: Stay informed about local regulations, entry requirements, and safety guidelines for your chosen destination. Check for any travel advisories or updates that may affect your day trip plans and be prepared to adapt as needed.

In summary, exploring the region surrounding Liechtenstein offers travelers a wealth of opportunities to discover new destinations, experience different cultures, and enjoy memorable adventures. Whether you're visiting historic cities, exploring natural landscapes, or indulging in culinary delights, day trips and excursions from Liechtenstein promise an unforgettable journey filled with exploration and discovery. So, pack your bags, lace up your shoes, and get ready to embark on an unforgettable journey through the heart of Europe.

Chapter 28
Sustainable Living: Environmental Initiatives

In today's world, the importance of sustainable living and environmental conservation cannot be overstated. As travelers, we have a responsibility to minimize our impact on the planet and contribute to the preservation of natural resources and ecosystems. In Liechtenstein, a small yet forward-thinking country nestled in the heart of the Alps, sustainability is not just a buzzword – it's a way of life. From renewable energy initiatives and waste reduction programs to eco-friendly transportation options and conservation efforts, Liechtenstein is leading the way in environmental stewardship and sustainable living. Join us as we explore some of the innovative initiatives and practices that make Liechtenstein a shining example of sustainability in action.

Renewable Energy: One of the cornerstones of Liechtenstein's sustainability efforts is its commitment to renewable energy sources. The principality boasts a diverse array of renewable energy projects, including hydroelectric power plants, solar installations, and biomass facilities. These renewable energy sources help reduce greenhouse gas emissions, decrease dependence on fossil fuels, and promote energy independence. In recent years, Liechtenstein has made significant investments in renewable energy infrastructure, with a goal of achieving carbon neutrality and transitioning to a fully sustainable energy system in the coming decades.

Waste Reduction and Recycling: Another key aspect of sustainable living in Liechtenstein is its comprehensive waste reduction and recycling programs. The principality places a strong emphasis on waste separation and recycling, with designated collection points for glass, paper, plastic, and organic waste throughout the country. Residents and businesses are encouraged to minimize waste generation through practices such as composting, reusable packaging, and conscious consumption. Additionally, Liechtenstein has implemented innovative recycling initiatives, such as bottle deposit systems and electronic waste recycling programs, to further reduce the environmental impact of waste disposal.

Eco-Friendly Transportation: In an effort to reduce carbon emissions and promote sustainable mobility, Liechtenstein has invested in eco-friendly transportation options for residents and visitors alike. The principality boasts an extensive network of cycling paths and pedestrian-friendly infrastructure, making it easy and convenient to explore the country on foot or by bike. Additionally, Liechtenstein offers efficient and environmentally friendly public transportation services, including buses and trains, which provide reliable connections to neighboring countries and destinations within the principality. For those seeking even greener options, electric vehicles and car-sharing programs are also available, offering a sustainable alternative to traditional gas-powered cars.

Conservation and Biodiversity: Despite its small size, Liechtenstein is home to a rich diversity of plant and animal species, many of which are protected by law and actively conserved through various conservation initiatives. The principality places a strong emphasis on preserving natural habitats, protecting endangered species, and promoting biodiversity conservation. Organizations such as the Liechtenstein Nature and Environment Foundation work tirelessly to safeguard the country's natural heritage through habitat restoration projects, species monitoring programs, and environmental education initiatives. Additionally, Liechtenstein's national parks and nature reserves provide valuable sanctuaries for wildlife and serve as important centers for research and conservation efforts.

Community Engagement and Education: Perhaps most importantly, sustainable living in Liechtenstein is not just a government-led initiative – it's a collective effort that involves active participation and engagement from the entire community. Residents, businesses, and organizations across the principality are committed to promoting environmental awareness, fostering sustainable practices, and inspiring positive change. Through educational programs, community events, and grassroots initiatives, Liechtenstein encourages individuals to take responsibility for their environmental footprint and make conscious choices that contribute to a healthier planet.

In conclusion, sustainable living and environmental conservation are deeply ingrained in the fabric of life in Liechtenstein. From renewable energy projects and waste reduction programs to eco-friendly transportation options and conservation efforts, the principality is leading by example in the global fight against climate change and environmental degradation. As travelers, we have the opportunity to learn from Liechtenstein's sustainability initiatives and incorporate eco-friendly practices into our own lives, both at home and on the road. By embracing sustainable living principles and supporting environmentally responsible businesses and destinations, we can all play a role in creating a more sustainable and resilient future for generations to come.

Chapter 29
Maintaining a Work-Life Balance

In today's fast-paced world, finding a balance between work and personal life can often feel like a daunting challenge. The demands of our professional responsibilities, combined with the desire to enjoy meaningful experiences and precious moments with loved ones, can sometimes leave us feeling overwhelmed and stretched thin. However, achieving a healthy work-life balance is not only essential for our well-being and happiness but also crucial for maintaining productivity, creativity, and overall satisfaction in both our personal and professional lives.

Understanding Work-Life Balance: Before we delve into strategies for achieving a harmonious work-life balance, let's first explore what this concept entails. At its core, work-life balance refers to the equilibrium between the time and energy we devote to our professional pursuits and the time and energy we allocate to our personal interests, relationships, and leisure activities. It's about prioritizing what matters most to us, setting boundaries, and making conscious choices that align with our values and goals. Achieving work-life balance is not about striving for perfection or completely eliminating stress from our lives but rather about finding a sustainable rhythm that allows us to thrive in all areas of our lives.

The Importance of Work-Life Balance: Maintaining a healthy work-life balance is essential for our physical, mental, and emotional well-being. When we neglect our personal lives in favor of work, we risk experiencing burnout, exhaustion, and diminished overall satisfaction. On the other hand, when we neglect our professional responsibilities in favor of personal pursuits, we may encounter setbacks, missed opportunities, and financial strain. By striking a balance between work and personal life, we can experience greater fulfillment, improved relationships, and enhanced overall quality of life.

Strategies for Achieving Work-Life Balance:

1. **Set Boundaries**: Establish clear boundaries between work and personal time to prevent work from encroaching on your personal life. Define specific work hours and stick to them as much as possible, avoiding the temptation to check emails or take work calls during your designated personal time.
2. **Prioritize Tasks**: Identify your most important tasks and prioritize them based on their level of urgency and importance. Focus on completing high-priority tasks during designated work hours, and avoid getting bogged down by less important or time-consuming tasks that can wait.
3. **Practice Time Management**: Utilize effective time management techniques, such as creating to-do lists, setting deadlines, and breaking tasks into smaller, manageable steps. By efficiently managing your time, you can maximize productivity during work hours and free up more time for leisure activities and personal pursuits.
4. **Delegate and Outsource**: Learn to delegate tasks that can be handled by others, whether it's assigning work responsibilities to colleagues or outsourcing household chores and errands. Delegating tasks allows you to focus on your core responsibilities and spend more time on activities that bring you joy and fulfillment.
5. **Schedule Downtime**: Make time for regular breaks and relaxation activities throughout the day to recharge and rejuvenate your mind and body. Whether it's taking a short walk, practicing mindfulness meditation, or enjoying a cup of tea, incorporating moments of relaxation into your daily routine can help reduce stress and improve overall well-being.

6. **Set Realistic Expectations**: Be realistic about what you can realistically accomplish within a given timeframe and avoid overcommitting yourself to too many tasks or obligations. Set achievable goals and expectations for yourself, and don't be afraid to say no to additional responsibilities when necessary.
7. **Disconnect from Technology**: Limit your exposure to digital devices and technology, especially outside of work hours. Set boundaries around checking emails, social media, and other digital distractions, and prioritize face-to-face interactions and quality time with loved ones.
8. **Invest in Self-Care**: Prioritize self-care activities that promote physical, mental, and emotional well-being, such as exercise, healthy eating, adequate sleep, and hobbies or interests that bring you joy. Taking care of yourself is essential for maintaining resilience and preventing burnout in both your personal and professional life.

Conclusion: Achieving a healthy work-life balance is an ongoing journey that requires self-awareness, intentionality, and commitment. By implementing strategies such as setting boundaries, prioritizing tasks, practicing time management, and investing in self-care, you can cultivate a more harmonious and fulfilling life that allows you to thrive both at work and at home. Remember that work-life balance looks different for everyone, so be patient with yourself as you navigate this journey and prioritize what matters most to you. By prioritizing your well-being and making conscious choices that align with your values and goals, you can create a life that is balanced, meaningful, and filled with joy and fulfillment.

Chapter 30
Dealing with Homesickness and Culture Shock

Embarking on a journey to a new country can be an exhilarating and transformative experience, filled with excitement, adventure, and discovery. However, along with the thrill of exploring unfamiliar landscapes and immersing oneself in different cultures, travelers may also encounter challenges such as homesickness and culture shock. These common experiences can arise when adjusting to life in a new environment, away from the comforts and familiarities of home. In this chapter, we'll explore strategies for coping with homesickness and culture shock, helping travelers navigate the ups and downs of living abroad with resilience and positivity.

Understanding Homesickness: Homesickness is a natural emotional response that can occur when individuals are separated from their home environment, loved ones, and familiar routines. It may manifest as feelings of sadness, loneliness, nostalgia, or longing for the comforts of home. Homesickness can be triggered by various factors, including cultural differences, language barriers, social isolation, and the challenges of adapting to a new way of life. While homesickness is a common experience among travelers, it's important to remember that it's temporary and can be managed effectively with the right strategies and support systems in place.

Coping with Homesickness:

1. **Stay Connected**: Maintain regular communication with friends and family back home through phone calls, video chats, emails, or social media. Sharing updates about your experiences and staying connected with loved ones can help alleviate feelings of isolation and loneliness.

2. **Establish Routines**: Create a sense of familiarity and structure in your daily life by establishing routines and rituals that bring comfort and stability. Whether it's enjoying a morning cup of coffee, going for a daily walk, or practicing a hobby or activity you enjoy, having consistent routines can help ground you during times of transition.
3. **Explore Your Surroundings**: Take advantage of opportunities to explore your new environment and immerse yourself in the local culture. Engage in activities that pique your curiosity, such as trying local cuisine, attending cultural events or festivals, or exploring nearby landmarks and attractions. Embracing new experiences can help you feel more connected to your surroundings and reduce feelings of homesickness.
4. **Build a Support Network**: Seek out opportunities to meet new people and build relationships with fellow expats, locals, or members of expat communities. Join social clubs, hobby groups, or language exchange programs where you can connect with like-minded individuals and forge meaningful connections. Having a support network of friends and peers can provide invaluable emotional support and companionship during your time abroad.
5. **Practice Self-Care**: Prioritize self-care practices that nourish your physical, mental, and emotional well-being. Make time for activities that help you relax, unwind, and recharge, such as exercise, meditation, journaling, or spending time outdoors in nature. Taking care of yourself is essential for coping with homesickness and maintaining resilience in the face of challenges.

Understanding Culture Shock: Culture shock is another common phenomenon experienced by travelers when adjusting to life in a new cultural environment. It occurs when individuals encounter unfamiliar customs, social norms, behaviors, and expectations that differ from those of their home culture. Culture shock can manifest in various ways, including feelings of frustration, confusion, disorientation, anxiety, or even hostility towards the host culture. While culture shock is a natural part of the acculturation process, it can be challenging to navigate without proper awareness and coping strategies.

Coping with Culture Shock:

1. **Educate Yourself**: Take the time to learn about the culture, customs, and traditions of your host country before and during your stay. Educating yourself about the local language, history, social norms, and cultural practices can help you better understand and navigate your new environment with respect and sensitivity.
2. **Maintain an Open Mind**: Approach cultural differences with an open mind and a willingness to learn and adapt. Be curious, ask questions, and embrace opportunities to engage with locals and immerse yourself in the local way of life. Keep in mind that cultural differences are not inherently good or bad – they are simply different, and understanding and respecting them is key to overcoming culture shock.
3. **Seek Cultural Immersion**: Actively seek out opportunities to immerse yourself in the local culture and engage in cultural exchange. Participate in cultural activities, attend cultural events or celebrations, and interact with locals in meaningful ways. Building bridges across cultural divides can help bridge the gap between yourself and the host culture and foster greater understanding and acceptance.
4. **Practice Patience and Flexibility**: Be patient with yourself and allow yourself time to adjust to your new surroundings. Understand that adaptation takes time and that it's normal to

experience ups and downs along the way. Practice flexibility and resilience in the face of challenges, and approach setbacks as learning opportunities rather than obstacles.

5. **Find Comfort in Familiarity**: While it's important to embrace new experiences and immerse yourself in the local culture, don't hesitate to seek out familiar comforts from home when needed. Whether it's cooking a favorite meal, listening to familiar music, or connecting with fellow expats, finding moments of familiarity can provide a sense of comfort and reassurance during times of culture shock.

Conclusion: Homesickness and culture shock are common challenges that many travelers face when adjusting to life in a new country. By understanding the underlying causes of these experiences and implementing effective coping strategies, travelers can navigate the ups and downs of living abroad with resilience, adaptability, and a positive outlook. Remember that homesickness and culture shock are temporary and manageable, and that with time, patience, and support, you can successfully overcome these challenges and thrive in your new cultural environment. Embrace the adventure of living abroad, and allow yourself to grow and evolve through the transformative journey of cultural immersion.

Chapter 31
Respecting Wildlife and Nature Conservation

As travelers, we have the privilege of exploring some of the most breathtaking natural landscapes and encountering fascinating wildlife species around the world. However, with this privilege comes a great responsibility to respect and protect the environment and its inhabitants. In this chapter, we'll delve into the importance of wildlife conservation and offer tips for travelers on how to minimize their impact on the natural world while enjoying their adventures.

Understanding Wildlife Conservation: Wildlife conservation is the practice of protecting and preserving the Earth's diverse array of plant and animal species, as well as their habitats. It is essential for maintaining biodiversity, ecosystem health, and the overall balance of nature. Many factors, including habitat destruction, pollution, climate change, poaching, and illegal wildlife trade, threaten the survival of wildlife species worldwide. Conservation efforts aim to address these threats and ensure the long-term survival of endangered species and their habitats.

The Importance of Wildlife Conservation:

1. **Biodiversity**: Wildlife conservation is essential for maintaining biodiversity, which refers to the variety of life forms on Earth. Biodiversity is crucial for ecosystem stability, resilience, and productivity, as well as for providing essential ecosystem services such as pollination, water purification, and nutrient cycling.
2. **Ecosystem Health**: Wildlife species play key roles in maintaining ecosystem health and functioning. They contribute to processes such as seed dispersal, predator-prey

interactions, and nutrient cycling, which are vital for the health and resilience of ecosystems. Protecting wildlife helps safeguard the health and integrity of entire ecosystems.
3. **Economic Benefits**: Wildlife conservation has significant economic benefits, including supporting ecotourism, providing recreational opportunities, and enhancing quality of life. Healthy ecosystems and diverse wildlife attract tourists and outdoor enthusiasts, contributing to local economies and providing livelihoods for communities that rely on nature-based tourism.
4. **Cultural Importance**: Many indigenous cultures around the world have deep spiritual, cultural, and traditional connections to wildlife and natural landscapes. Wildlife conservation helps preserve cultural heritage and traditions, as well as the cultural identities of indigenous peoples who depend on natural resources for their livelihoods and cultural practices.

Tips for Respecting Wildlife and Nature Conservation:

1. **Observe Wildlife Responsibly**: When encountering wildlife in their natural habitats, maintain a safe distance and observe from a respectful distance. Avoid disturbing or approaching animals too closely, as this can cause stress, disrupt natural behaviors, and pose safety risks for both you and the animals.
2. **Leave No Trace**: Practice Leave No Trace principles when exploring natural areas, including parks, reserves, and wilderness areas. Pack out all trash and litter, minimize campfire impacts, stay on designated trails, and avoid trampling vegetation or disturbing sensitive habitats.
3. **Support Conservation Initiatives**: Contribute to wildlife conservation efforts by supporting organizations and initiatives that work to protect endangered species and their

habitats. Consider donating to conservation charities, volunteering for wildlife monitoring or habitat restoration projects, or participating in ecotourism activities that support local conservation efforts.
4. **Respect Wildlife Laws and Regulations**: Familiarize yourself with wildlife protection laws and regulations in the areas you visit, and adhere to them at all times. Observe wildlife viewing guidelines, obtain necessary permits for activities such as fishing or birdwatching, and refrain from engaging in activities that harm or exploit wildlife.
5. **Educate Yourself and Others**: Take the time to educate yourself about the wildlife species and ecosystems you encounter during your travels. Learn about their behaviors, habitats, and conservation status, and share this knowledge with others to raise awareness about the importance of wildlife conservation.
6. **Choose Responsible Tour Operators**: When participating in wildlife-related activities such as safaris, snorkeling, or whale watching, choose tour operators that prioritize ethical and sustainable practices. Look for operators that follow wildlife viewing guidelines, respect animal welfare standards, and support local conservation initiatives.

Conclusion: Respecting wildlife and supporting nature conservation are essential responsibilities for travelers who seek to explore and enjoy the natural world responsibly. By practicing responsible wildlife viewing, minimizing our environmental impact, supporting conservation initiatives, and educating ourselves and others about the importance of wildlife conservation, we can all play a role in protecting and preserving the Earth's precious biodiversity for future generations to enjoy. Let's embrace our role as stewards of the natural world and take meaningful action to ensure that wildlife and wild places thrive for years to come.

Chapter 32

Celebrating Diversity: Expat Communities in Liechtenstein

Nestled between Switzerland and Austria, Liechtenstein may be one of the world's smallest countries, but it boasts a vibrant and diverse expat community that adds richness and flavor to its cultural tapestry. From skilled professionals and entrepreneurs to students and retirees, expatriates from around the globe have chosen to make Liechtenstein their home for various reasons, contributing their unique perspectives, talents, and traditions to the principality's multicultural landscape. In this chapter, we'll explore the dynamic expat communities in Liechtenstein, highlighting the experiences, challenges, and opportunities that come with living as an expatriate in this charming Alpine nation.

The Expatriate Experience in Liechtenstein:

Living as an expatriate in Liechtenstein offers a unique blend of opportunities and challenges, as individuals navigate the intricacies of adapting to a new culture, language, and way of life. For many expats, the decision to relocate to Liechtenstein is driven by factors such as career opportunities, quality of life, safety, and proximity to nature. The principality's stable economy, low crime rate, and stunning natural scenery make it an attractive destination for those seeking a high standard of living in a picturesque setting.

Expat Communities and Networks:

Despite its small size, Liechtenstein is home to a diverse array of expatriate communities representing countries from around the world. Expats from Europe, Asia, the Americas, and beyond come together to form close-knit communities and support networks, providing social, professional, and cultural connections for newcomers and long-term residents alike. Whether through expat clubs, language exchange programs, cultural associations, or community events, expatriates in

Liechtenstein have ample opportunities to connect with others, share experiences, and forge friendships that transcend borders.

Professional Opportunities:

Liechtenstein's robust economy and business-friendly environment make it an attractive destination for skilled professionals and entrepreneurs seeking career opportunities in various sectors, including finance, technology, manufacturing, and healthcare. Expatriates working in Liechtenstein benefit from competitive salaries, favorable tax policies, and a strong support network of multinational companies, professional associations, and business incubators. Additionally, the principality's central location in Europe and its proximity to major economic hubs like Zurich and Munich make it a strategic base for international business activities and networking opportunities.

Cultural Exchange and Integration:

One of the most enriching aspects of living as an expatriate in Liechtenstein is the opportunity for cultural exchange and integration. Expats have the chance to immerse themselves in Liechtenstein's rich cultural heritage, traditions, and customs, while also sharing their own cultural backgrounds and traditions with the local community. Whether through participating in local festivals and celebrations, attending cultural events, or volunteering for community initiatives, expatriates play an active role in promoting cross-cultural understanding and appreciation in Liechtenstein.

Challenges of Expat Life:

While expatriate life in Liechtenstein offers many rewards, it also comes with its fair share of challenges. Adapting to a new language, navigating bureaucratic procedures, and adjusting to cultural differences can be daunting tasks for newcomers. Additionally, expatriates may experience feelings of homesickness, social isolation, or cultural adjustment stress as they acclimate to their new environment. However, with resilience, flexibility, and a positive attitude, many expats find ways to overcome these challenges and thrive in their adopted homeland.

Conclusion:

The expatriate communities in Liechtenstein are vibrant, diverse, and welcoming, reflecting the principality's commitment to embracing cultural diversity and fostering a sense of belonging for all residents. Whether you're a newcomer embarking on your expat journey or a long-term resident looking to connect with others, Liechtenstein offers a supportive and inclusive environment where individuals from around the world can come together, share experiences, and build meaningful connections. As you explore the expat communities in Liechtenstein, embrace the opportunity to learn from others, celebrate diversity, and contribute your own unique perspective to the tapestry of expatriate life in this charming Alpine nation.

Conclusion

As you reach the end of this comprehensive guide to moving to Liechtenstein, it's time to reflect on the wealth of information you've encountered and the exciting journey that lies ahead. Whether you're considering a move to this tiny Alpine nation for work, study, retirement, or simply to explore its natural beauty and rich cultural heritage, you're embarking on an adventure filled with opportunities for growth, discovery, and new experiences.

Liechtenstein, despite its small size, offers a wealth of attractions and amenities that cater to a diverse range of interests and lifestyles. From its stunning mountain landscapes and pristine alpine lakes to its vibrant cultural scene and thriving expatriate communities, the principality has something to offer everyone who calls it home. Whether you're drawn to the tranquility of its natural surroundings, the allure of its economic opportunities, or the charm of its historic towns and villages, Liechtenstein has a way of capturing the hearts of all who visit.

Throughout this guide, we've covered a wide range of topics aimed at helping you navigate the practicalities of moving to and living in Liechtenstein. From understanding residency requirements and finding accommodation to navigating the healthcare system, education options, and employment opportunities, we've provided you with valuable insights and practical advice to facilitate a smooth transition to life in the principality. Additionally, we've explored the rich cultural tapestry of Liechtenstein, from its diverse expatriate communities and vibrant festivals to its delectable cuisine and thriving arts scene.

As you prepare to embark on your journey to Liechtenstein, it's important to approach the experience with an open mind, a spirit of adventure, and a willingness to embrace the unknown. Moving to a new country, whether temporarily or permanently, can be both exhilarating and challenging, filled with moments of excitement, wonder, and occasional moments of homesickness or culture shock. However, it's through these experiences that we grow, learn, and ultimately thrive in our new surroundings.

As you settle into life in Liechtenstein, take the time to explore your new environment, connect with the local community, and immerse yourself in the rich tapestry of culture, history, and natural beauty that the principality has to offer. Whether you find yourself hiking through the picturesque Alps, sampling delicious local cuisine, or forging friendships with fellow expatriates and locals alike, cherish each moment and embrace the opportunity to create lasting memories in your new home.

Remember that adjusting to life in a new country takes time, patience, and resilience, and it's okay to seek support and guidance along the way. Whether you're grappling with language barriers, navigating bureaucratic procedures, or simply feeling homesick for familiar comforts, know that you're not alone. Reach out to fellow expatriates, local support networks, and resources available to you, and don't hesitate to ask for help when you need it.

As you embark on this new chapter of your life in Liechtenstein, may you find joy, fulfillment, and a sense of belonging in your new surroundings. Whether you're drawn to the pristine natural landscapes, the dynamic cultural scene, or the welcoming embrace of the local community, may your journey be filled with adventure, discovery, and endless possibilities. Welcome to Liechtenstein – your gateway to a world of opportunity and adventure awaits.

Appendix

Congratulations on reaching the appendix of this comprehensive guide to moving to Liechtenstein! Here, you'll find a wealth of additional resources, practical tips, and useful information to supplement your journey to the charming Alpine principality. Whether you're seeking further guidance on specific topics, looking for additional resources to aid in your transition, or simply curious to learn more about Liechtenstein, this appendix is designed to provide you with valuable insights and assistance as you prepare for your adventure.

Useful Contacts and Resources:

1. **Embassies and Consulates**: Contact information for embassies and consulates representing your home country in Liechtenstein, as well as those of other countries you may wish to visit or engage with during your time in the principality.
2. **Government Offices**: Contact details for relevant government offices in Liechtenstein, including immigration authorities, tax offices, and municipal administrations, to assist with residency applications, permits, and other administrative matters.
3. **Chambers of Commerce and Business Associations**: Information on chambers of commerce, industry associations, and business networks in Liechtenstein, offering support and resources for entrepreneurs, investors, and professionals seeking to do business in the principality.
4. **Community and Expat Organizations**: Contact information for expatriate organizations, social clubs, and community groups in Liechtenstein, providing opportunities for networking, cultural exchange, and social activities with fellow expats and locals.

5. **Language Schools and Cultural Institutes**: Listings of language schools, cultural institutes, and language exchange programs in Liechtenstein, offering language courses, cultural immersion experiences, and opportunities to learn German or other languages spoken in the principality.
6. **Healthcare Providers and Services**: Directory of healthcare providers, hospitals, clinics, and medical services in Liechtenstein, including information on health insurance coverage, emergency services, and medical specialists.
7. **Education Institutions**: Information on schools, universities, and educational institutions in Liechtenstein, including international schools, vocational training centers, and higher education institutions offering degree programs in various fields.
8. **Legal and Financial Advisors**: Listings of legal firms, financial advisors, and consultants in Liechtenstein, offering expertise in areas such as tax planning, estate planning, immigration law, and business regulations.

Practical Tips and Advice:

1. **Currency and Banking**: Tips for managing your finances in Liechtenstein, including information on currency exchange, banking services, and opening a bank account in the principality.
2. **Transportation**: Guidance on navigating transportation options in Liechtenstein, including public transportation, driving regulations, car rental services, and bicycle infrastructure.
3. **Housing and Accommodation**: Advice on finding housing and accommodation in Liechtenstein, including rental listings, real estate agencies, and tips for negotiating rental agreements.

4. **Shopping and Services**: Information on shopping facilities, supermarkets, specialty stores, and essential services in Liechtenstein, as well as tips for shopping responsibly and supporting local businesses.
5. **Entertainment and Recreation**: Suggestions for leisure activities, cultural attractions, and recreational pursuits in Liechtenstein, including outdoor adventures, cultural events, and entertainment venues.
6. **Emergency Services and Safety**: Guidance on accessing emergency services, including police, fire, and medical assistance, as well as tips for staying safe and aware of potential risks in Liechtenstein.

Additional Information:

1. **Travel Tips**: Practical advice and recommendations for travelers visiting Liechtenstein, including visa requirements, travel insurance, packing tips, and cultural etiquette.
2. **Useful Websites and Online Resources**: Links to websites, online forums, and social media groups providing information, support, and community for expatriates and travelers in Liechtenstein.
3. **Recommended Reading**: A selection of books, articles, and publications about Liechtenstein's history, culture, and society, offering further insights into the principality's unique identity and heritage.
4. **Glossary of Terms**: Definitions of key terms and terminology relevant to life in Liechtenstein, including terms related to residency, immigration, healthcare, education, and legal matters.

Conclusion:

As you explore the resources and information provided in this appendix, I hope you feel more equipped and prepared for your journey to Liechtenstein. Whether you're embarking on a new chapter in your life, pursuing career opportunities, or simply seeking adventure in a new environment, may your time in the principality be filled with excitement, growth, and memorable experiences. Remember to embrace the challenges and opportunities that come your way, and don't hesitate to reach out for support and assistance when needed. Welcome to Liechtenstein – your gateway to a world of possibilities awaits!

Printed in Great Britain
by Amazon